Karla Faye Tucker
SET FREE

Life and Faith on Death Row

Linda Strom

SHAW

WATERBROOK
PRESS

KARLA FAYE TUCKER SET FREE
PUBLISHED BY WATERBROOK PRESS
12265 Oracle Boulevard, Suite 200
Colorado Springs, Colorado 80921

All Scripture quotations, unless otherwise indicated, are taken from the *Holy Bible, New International Version* ®. NIV®. Copyright © 1973, 1978, 1984 by International Bible Society. Used by permission of Zondervan Publishing House. All rights reserved. Scripture quotations marked (TLB) are taken from The Living Bible copyright © 1971. Used by permission of Tyndale House Publishers, Inc., Wheaton, Illinois 60189. All rights reserved. Scripture quotations marked (MSG) are taken from The Message by Eugene H. Peterson. Copyright © 1993, 1994, 1995, 1996, 2000, 2001, 2002. Used by permission of NavPress Publishing Group. All rights reserved. Scripture quotations marked (RSV) are taken from the Revised Standard Version of the Bible, copyright © 1952 [2nd edition, 1971] by the Division of Christian Education of the National Council of the Churches of Christ in the USA. Used by permission. All rights reserved. Scripture quotations marked (NLT) are taken from the Holy Bible, New Living Translation, copyright © 1996. Used by permission of Tyndale House Publishers Inc., Wheaton, Illinois 60189. All rights reserved.

Italicized words in Scripture quotations reflect the author's emphasis.

Excerpts from "You Are My All in All" by Dennis Jernigan used by permission.
"Hope of Heaven" by Mario Bergner used by permission.

ISBN 978-0-307-72978-1

Photographs on pages 14, 46 (top), 68 (top), 144, 160, 176, 192, 230, and 234 by Ron Kuntz.

We have sought to secure permission for all copyrighted material in this book. Where acknowledgment was inadvertently omitted the publisher expresses regret.

Published in the United States by WaterBrook Multnomah, an imprint of the Crown Publishing Group, a division of Random House Inc., New York.

Printed in the United States of America
2010

10 9 8 7 6 5 4 3 2 1

This book made available without charge by The 1687 Foundation, a nonprofit, tax exempt organization dedicated to advancing spiritual and charitable purposes. Please note that these books may only be given away. They cannot be sold, cannot be used to raise money, and cannot be a "free giveaway" for any commercial or personal-gain purpose whatsoever.
For additional information, please contact:
info@1687foundation.com
Tel: 541.549.7600
Fax: 541.549.7603

Dedication

To Stephen Leonard Strom,
born January 24th, 1998,
eight days before Karla Faye Tucker was executed.
The angels danced the day you were born,
my precious grandson.

And to Karla Faye Tucker.
On February 3, 1998, you joined the angels
in their dance. How we miss you,
our compassionate friend.
Keep the party going—we're on our way.

About the Author

Linda Strom and her husband Dallas are the founders of Discipleship Unlimited, a healing ministry that reaches out to prisoners, their families, and others in need of healing. DU is a nonprofit organization run by volunteers from across the country. Linda is a contributor to *Just Between Friends* by Terry Meeuwsen. Linda and Dallas have three children and two grandchildren.

For more information about Discipleship Unlimited, please visit our website at www.liferow.org or write:

Discipleship Unlimited
P.O. Box 145
Gatesville, TX 76528

All author proceeds from Karla Faye Tucker Set Free *will go to Discipleship Unlimited.*

Contents

Foreword

Blessed are the pure of heart, for they shall see God" (Matthew 5:8). The essence of purity is to be free from deceit, having sincerity of heart. Karla Faye Tucker was "pure of heart." That may be hard for some people to accept if they only focused on where she came from and what she had done. Karla's background was disastrous; her crime, violent and horrendous. But if you're looking for a shocking tale filled with gory details, you've come to the wrong place. This is a story of redemption! This is the love story of a woman imprisoned by her circumstances, her choices, and the law. A woman who found a freedom so all-encompassing that she could soar above it all—even imprisonment and her own pending death.

I came to know Karla long before I actually met her. My friend, Linda Strom, had been Karla's spiritual advisor for many years. Each time Linda came back from ministering in the prison at Gatesville, she would bring news of her friends on "Life Row." Nothing could have prepared me, however, for the intense feelings that meeting Karla stirred up in my heart when I met her in person. What was it about this Death-Row inmate about to face execution that made me feel so captivated? Guards, gates, steel doors, and heavy mesh surrounded and separated us, yet I felt so drawn to this intense woman who was alive with joy and enveloped with peace. The presence of God seemed almost tangible.

Though Karla was locked up on Death Row, I don't

think any of us really believed she would ever be executed. So loving, so vivacious, so full of grace—surely she'd be pardoned. And yet, the more imminent the reality of the death sentence became, and the closer the execution date, the more we saw Karla's face aglow with the love of her Lord. For Linda, who loved Karla so deeply, it was a time of personal spiritual surrender mixed with unending hope and a growing grief. Karla was like a daughter to Linda. Letting go is always hard.

Jesus said He came to set the captives free. Karla received that invitation. She was freer than most of us because she put aside anything that would have hindered her walk with Jesus. Though she treasured her friends, she drew her strength and peace from Him. It was a spiritual adventure that radically changed her life and the lives of everyone who came to know her.

As you read her story, listen with your heart for the message that Karla longed to share with anyone who was willing to listen... *"the one the Son sets free, is free indeed!"*

Terry Meeuwsen
Co-host, *The 700 Club*

Acknowledgments

When I began writing *Karla Faye Tucker Set Free* my husband invited me out for a romantic breakfast. After I got my morning coffee, he handed me an envelope. I thought that he'd gotten our anniversary mixed up until I opened it. On the card, a toddler, in rolled-up bib overalls and an oversized red shirt, is climbing over the bottom rung of a wooden fence. What an illustration of determination! Printed inside were the words, "I know you can do it!" and underneath, Dallas's handwritten note: "I love you," signed "Big D."

I'm a visionary and I dream big dreams. I also know how much I need other people in my life to help achieve those dreams. Whenever I get a new inspiration, Dallas looks at me and says, "What fence are we painting now, Tom Sawyer?"

As we sat over our coffee that morning, Dallas and I talked about the book and how it was birthed. During an early morning breakfast at our October 1998 "Healing for Your Heart" conference in Milwaukee, Wisconsin, editor Janet Thoma challenged me to write a book. Exhaustion from the conference lifted as I envisioned telling readers about Karla Faye Tucker and the many lives influenced by her fearless faith and disarming love. In the beginning it was a huge, unpainted fence; now I want to thank the many who helped paint it!

Janet Thoma, thank you for calling forth this book and for the time you spent working with me.

Donna Dixon, you have constantly been by my side, paintbrush in hand. I cannot begin to thank you, and yet I know you have loved every minute of it. We have prayed over this manuscript chapter by chapter, and you have patiently reworked each with me. You are humble and gifted, but most important, you are also my friend.

Special thanks to Harold Shaw Publishers: to Elisa Fryling for affirming the vision, to Joan Guest for pressing for excellence, and to Bob Bittner for his patience and encouragement.

Thanks to the Discipleship Unlimited team who cheered, prayed, and believed that this book would be published.

Ron Kuntz—for over two decades your skill as a photographer has been a treasure to those inside more than 500 prisons. Thank you for going into Gatesville's Mountain View Unit to take those beautiful photos of Karla two months before her execution. Prominently placed on the fireplace mantle in my living room is one of my most treasured possessions—your last picture of Karla.

Pam Perillo, Death Row inmate 665, Mountain View Unit, Gatesville, Texas—thank you for the letters and stories you've shared, and most of all for your love for Karla. Pam, I love you and pray this book will somehow make sense of the pain in your life. May you begin to understand the extent of the impact the women on the Row have made in the lives of those who've walked through its door.

Frances Newton, Death Row inmate 922, Mountain View Unit—you are a mighty woman of valor! Karla considered you not only her friend but also her prayer partner. Thank you for sharing your life and the letters Karla sent you.

Fran Turner, inmate 371487 and prison beautician at Mountain View Unit—you are a gifted writer. The letters you sent describing your friendship with Karla deeply touched me. The precious scenes you created will remain in my heart forever.

To all the other men and women behind the fences: I confess this is my best effort to communicate Karla's love for you. Far more important, and I know she'd agree, is the great value our Father places on your lives.

I know Karla would want to thank the many volunteers and prison ministry groups that faithfully reach out to those in physical and spiritual prisons. God uses your efforts to change lives. Thank you.

And to Karla Faye Tucker, one who knew how to give out God's love by the bucketful to all of us, this one's for you!

Part I

The Road to Death Row

Karla in the yard outside Death Row at the Gatesville Mountain View Unit.

Chapter One

Inmate 777

When I share that I was out of it on drugs the night I brutally murdered two people, I fully realize that I made the choice to do those drugs. Had I chosen not to do drugs, two people would still be alive today. But I did choose to do drugs, and I did lose it, and two people are dead because of me.

--Karla Faye Tucker in her letter to Governor Bush and the Texas Board of Pardons and Paroles, January 1998

If anyone is in Christ, he is a new creation; the old has gone, the new has come!

—2 Corinthians 5:17

February 3, 1998, 6:25 P.M., Walls Unit, Huntsville, Texas

With the strength and poise of a gymnast, Karla leapt up on the gurney and whispered a prayer: "Lord Jesus, help them to find my vein." Then, strapped to the table, she looked toward the small window and spoke her last words.

"Can Warden Baggett hear me?"

15

After being assured that yes, the warden was nearby and was listening, Karla went on: "I would like to say to all of you—the Thornton family and Jerry Dean's family—that I am so sorry. I hope God will give you peace with this.

"Baby, I love you," she told her husband, Dana. "Ron, give Peggy a hug for me. Everybody has been so good to me. I love all of you very much. I'm going to be face to face with Jesus now.

"Warden Baggett, thank you so much. You have been so good to me. I love all of you very much. I will see you all when you get there. I will wait for you."

After her final words she licked her lips and, according to witnesses, appeared to be humming softly as she waited for the lethal injection.

◆ ◆ ◆

"Karla, how do you explain to yourself that you were involved in a violent slaying?" television interviewer Larry King asked, his familiar face separated from hers by a scratched Plexiglas window.

Millions of viewers throughout the world were riveted to their television sets in January 1998 as the drama unfolded on CNN's *Larry King Live*. They, too, wanted to know the answer. Who was this attractive and captivating woman that drew Larry to Texas? How could she have committed such a heinous crime?

Pausing just for an instant, Karla looked steadily back at him. "I can't make sense out of it, Larry. I don't know how to answer, except to say that because of the choices

I made to do drugs and buckle to peer pressure, it was inevitable that something like that was going to happen in my life."

While they continued talking and the CNN camera crew filmed the interview, I sat in the chapel at Karla's prison, praying. After it was over, Karla and I would meet for our daily two-hour visit. As I waited, I thought about the events that had led her to this place.

❖ ❖ ❖

Over the years I'd heard much about Karla's life. While never shy, she shared her story with me cautiously. She never hesitated to accept responsibility for what she had done. Better than anyone, she knew the horrific life from which she'd now been set free.

When she talked with reporters she carefully omitted details about the crime itself. "I think about it pretty often; I am well aware of what I have done. But it's pretty hard to talk about because it brings up too many painful memories. I think about the pain I put others through. I wish it had never happened. If I could go back, I would not do it again. Now I know the value of human life."

She understood that each time her victims' family or members of her own family read or saw anything about the crime, they experienced renewed grief. In addition to not wanting to relive the past herself, she wanted to spare them as much pain as possible.

I feel the same way. The two murders Karla committed were a tragedy; the lives of everyone connected will never be the same. Yet, the Karla I had come to know was not the same young woman who had committed the crime. She had been transformed—as I am being transformed—by a relationship with Jesus Christ.

❖ ❖ ❖

Karla Faye Tucker was born November 18, 1959, in Houston, Texas. "As a little girl, I remember that we were a family," Karla said when I asked about her background. "We lived in a middle-class neighborhood and went to the bay house where we water-skied and fished. But that period didn't last very long. My parents fought a lot and divorced each other several times."

As her parents' turmoil increased, Karla's life began unraveling. Her first experience with drugs came when she was seven or eight. "I caught [my older sisters] smoking pot and threatened to tell our parents," she told the *Gatesville Messenger* in 1998 (January 30). "But they gave it to me and then said I couldn't tell because I was doing it too."

Karla remembered one brief encounter with what seemed to be a normal life. "At school this little girl would talk to me. I remember seeing something really different in her. It was like a genuine love for people. But her parents didn't want her hanging around with me because they thought that I was just a bad, bad child.

"Somewhere along the way she talked her mother into letting me go to church with them. I think they must have been [very conservative] because they wore something on their heads and had to wear dresses. We sat on the front row. At some point she was down on her knees and really praying in the Spirit. I thought, *What is going on here?* Everybody came and laid their hands on her. I don't remember doing anything wrong that night, but they never would talk to me again. Why didn't they reach out to me? Why did they cut me off?"

Life at home was rapidly deteriorating. Any chance of a normal childhood disintegrated. "Back then there was a lot of drugs and sex. My sisters ran around with older people. One of their friends was in a biker club. He came to see my sisters and when he found out they weren't there, he took me off on his motorcycle. He asked me if I wanted to shoot some heroin. I think he was going to molest me. But he shot me so full of heroin that I got sick and he wasn't able to do anything. He ended up dropping me off at some apartments. That was the beginning of me shooting dope."

By the time Karla was in seventh grade she was heavily into drugs and she dropped out of school. "I got kicked out as much as quit," she said. When her parents divorced for the last time, she chose to live with her mother, Carolyn Moore. Life with her mom was unrestricted, with little or no adult supervision.

"There were a couple of things my mother did that made me wonder, *Don't you see what you are doing to me? Why don't you notice this and come to me and ask what is going on?*" In spite of inner turmoil and confusion, Karla wanted to be just like her mother. When Karla was only fourteen she followed her mother into prostitution.

When Karla was about sixteen years old she met Stephen Griffith. In a *Houston Chronicle* article published on the day of Karla's execution, Griffith described their relationship.

"I was nineteen years old. I had a Harley-Davidson, worked six months a year, and made $20,000. I thought I was on top of the world. Me and a bunch of buddies pulled into a local park. We were hanging out and partying. Karla Faye and one of her friends were over there smoking a fat, pink joint. I hollered over and introduced myself. That's how we met."

About a year later, they married. "We got along fairly well," Griffith said. "We fist-fought a lot. I've never had men hit me as hard as she did. Whenever I went into a bar, I didn't have to worry because she had my back covered. She was tough." For fun, the couple collected guns, joined a motorcycle club, and played tackle football without protective gear.

"I saw things in her that no one else did," Griffith said. "That girl had so much potential. She could talk to anyone and make them feel at ease. She was charismatic. Even when she was on drugs and could hardly walk, she was beautiful." Griffith himself had serious substance-abuse problems. Still, he described Karla as "a pretty good wife": she cleaned the house, got him off to work on time, and fixed his meals.

When Karla announced she was leaving Griffith to work out her "wild streak," he feared the worst. "When we split, I told my friend she was going to get killed or kill somebody."

Once separated from her husband, Karla continued downward in her life of drugs and prostitution. Periodically, over a span of several years, she was one of the groupies following the Allman Brothers Band. In 1981 she met Jerry Lynn Dean when he was involved with her best friend and roommate, Shawn. From the beginning, their relationship was turbulent. The animosity between them developed over the next two years. By 1983, Karla was living with a man named Danny Garret in a tumultuous household where drugs, sex, and physical fights were the norm. She was the group's leader.

On June 11, Karla, her sister, and their friends decided to celebrate her sister's birthday with a weekend bash. From Friday through Sunday they sat around the house shooting heroin, smoking cocaine, and popping massive quantities of other illegal drugs.

It was then—high on drugs, sleep-deprived, and talking about old grudges— that Karla and Danny decided to drive over to Jerry Dean's apartment and case it out in the hope of stealing his motorcycle. They weren't expecting him to be home. However, Jerry Dean and Deborah Thornton, who had just met that afternoon at a party, were asleep in the bedroom. At about 3:00 A.M. on June 13, 1983, Danny and Karla silently entered the apartment.

Something went horribly wrong. Instead of stealing a motorcycle, Danny and Karla murdered two people. Just weeks after Karla's marriage to Stephen Griffith officially ended in divorce, Karla Faye Tucker was charged with the pickax murders of Jerry Lynn Dean and Deborah Thornton.

❖ ❖ ❖

Testimony in Karla's trial began on April 11, 1984. After only seventy minutes of deliberation, Karla was found guilty of capital murder by an eight-woman, four-man jury.

The Karla who testified in court, however, was dramatically different from the woman who had committed a heinous crime months earlier. While awaiting trial, Karla had come to have a faith in Jesus Christ and His redemption. A remarkable change in her had taken place. The cold-blooded killer who had hidden from authorities became a repentant and emotional woman who confessed to the murders she had committed, testifying during the punishment phase of her trial that even being pickaxed herself would be insufficient to atone for her crime.

Because of Karla's open confession, her conviction was swift. Legal deliberations in Karla's case, though, continued for the next fourteen years:

- April 11, 1984: Karla was found guilty of capital murder.

- April 25, 1984: Karla was sentenced to death.

- October 9, 1984: Danny Garret's trial for Deborah's murder began.

- October 30, 1984: Karla turned state's witness and testified against Danny. (Danny later was sentenced to death. He died of liver disease while in prison.)

- June 24, 1987: Karla's attorneys asked the Texas Court of Criminal Appeals to reverse her conviction.

- December 7, 1988: The court upheld her conviction.

- June 26, 1989: The U.S. Supreme Court refused to hear her appeal.

- February 27, 1992: Texas State District Judge Pat Lykos rejected Karla's request for a hearing to present new evidence.

- May 29, 1992: Judge Lykos set Karla's first execution date for June 30, 1992. On June 22, the Court of Appeals stayed (stopped) the execution.

- October 21, 1993: Even though a Court of Appeals stay was in effect, Judge Lykos set a November 19, 1993 execution date. On November 9, the Court of Appeals reinstated Karla's indefinite stay of execution.

- January 30, 1995: The Court of Appeals lifted the stay of execution and denied the opportunity to appeal.

- August 3, 1995: Citing new evidence in her case, Karla's attorneys petitioned the federal court for an evidentiary hearing. They were unsuccessful.

- December 8, 1997: The U.S. Supreme Court rejected the attorneys' request to review the case.

- December 18, 1997: Texas State District Judge Debbie Stricklin set Karla's execution for February 3, 1998.

- January 20, 1998: Karla's attorneys asked the Court of Appeals to postpone her execution to give them time to challenge the state's clemency procedure.

- January 22, 1998: Karla officially asked the Texas Board of Pardons and Paroles to commute her punishment from death to life imprisonment. She also asked Governor George W. Bush to postpone her execution thirty days.

- January 28, 1998: Her requests were denied.

- February 3, 1998: Karla was executed by lethal injection.

The well-known facts of Karla's case cannot begin to tell the story of her life "behind the fences." This book reveals a new story, the story of how God transforms lives. This is not only Karla's story, but the stories of the many people God touched through her. It is really God's story. It was God who saw that lonely little girl sitting in the front row of a small church in Texas. It was God who transformed a hardened murderer to a joyful, gentle young woman. It was God who gave Karla the longing for the completeness that her inmate number suggested: 777, the biblical number for wholeness and perfection. And it was God who reached countless individuals through Karla's life and testimony.

As Larry King's intense, hour-long interview ended that January evening, he paused, looked at Karla and said, "Finally, you remain up."

"Yes."

"Can you explain that to me a little bit more? It can't just be God."

Karla smiled broadly. "Yes, it can. It's called the joy of the Lord. When you've done something like I've done and you've been forgiven for it and you're loved—that has a way of so changing you. I have experienced real love. I know what forgiveness is, even when I've done something so horrible. I know that because God forgave me when I accepted what Jesus did on the cross. When I leave here I'm going to be with Him."

The author and her husband, Dallas, in February 1998.

Chapter Two

I'll Walk You Home

Never will I leave you; never will I forsake you.

—*Hebrews 13:5b*

I am literally weeping at this very moment as I think about how year after year I have seen your ministry team walk in here and see people. You reach out from your own broken, bruised, and battered experiences and you do surgery and it just blows me away. God flows and heals people and that is so necessary before a person can really open up and flower.

—*Karla Faye Tucker, in a letter to the author*

When I first went to Mountain View Prison in Gatesville, Texas, in 1987, I knew little about Karla Faye Tucker. I knew little, in fact, about Texas. This became quickly apparent to others when my friend Rosalie Shidler and I rode into the small, southwestern town in a rented, bright-red Cadillac. Rosalie, whose hair was bleached blonde, was dressed in a hot-pink Liz Claiborne silk pantsuit. We walked into Andy's Restaurant, a local family dining spot, and she strolled up to the hostess station, "A non, please."

I knew "non" meant "nonsmoking section," but the

hostess didn't, and neither did two tall, burly men dressed in cowboy boots and Stetsons.

The cowboys knew we had come to town.

We were going to Mountain View Prison to conduct a seminar for the six hundred women incarcerated there. Rosalie believed that the Lord had called her to be my prayer partner, to travel with me whenever she could, at her own expense. Other volunteers would come from Waco, Texas, to lead singing and to participate in small groups.

I was glad Rosalie was with me. I knew I needed her prayer support when I had talked to Chaplain Tim Crosby during an earlier phone call. He had said, "I'd like you to teach the Prison Fellowship module 'You Are Somebody.' Many inmates have experienced a lot of abuse. Others are trying to face their pain and guilt because they're separated from their children. Then there is the lesbian issue. The key to their healing is accepting who they are in Christ."

He offered other guidelines, one of which was, "Do not wear white. The inmates wear white uniforms, and during count you will confuse the guards if you do too."

Chaplain Crosby told me we could expect maybe fifty inmates at the seminar, but that Friday evening the women just kept coming in, one hundred in all. Many walked past me with dull, blank expressions. Some inmates were sent here for petty crimes such as writing bad checks. Others were here for major offenses such as theft and murder, many of which were alcohol or drug related.

Going into prison is always an exhilarating experience

for me, not a fearful one. It's a deep call in my heart, since I know what it's like to live in an emotional prison and feel there is no way out. It's exciting to know that Jesus can set these women free. As the women began sitting down in the well-worn pews, I felt like a horse straining against the starting gate before a race. This weekend seminar at Mountain View Prison was to change the direction of my life.

The meeting began with music, but it was soon interrupted. An officer walked onto the platform and shouted, "Count time!" I glanced around at the women, startled by the quiet. I was also struck by the whiteness of everyone's clothing, including my own. Then it hit me. I couldn't believe what I had done. I was dressed in a white sweater and slacks, which closely resembled the prison uniform. Chaplain Crosby had warned me not to wear white, but when someone tells me not to do something, sometimes I unintentionally end up doing just the opposite.

I knew I had to move because I was sitting among the inmates. I also knew there was no way to be subtle about this. The prison count would be off if I didn't move. We were sitting in church pews, each with a paper label on the end. On the right side of the chapel were A1, B1, C1, and on through H1. On the left side, A2, B2, C2, etc., representing the general prison population housed in dorms.

"Dorm A1!" the officer yelled.

All the women-in-white in the first row on the right side stood up to be counted. The guard scribbled numbers on a paper attached to a clipboard.

"Dorm A2!"

All the women-in-white in the first row on the left side stood. Again the guard scribbled the count.

"Dorm B1!"

All the women-in-white in the second row, right side, stood.

Since I was sitting in the third row I had to move— now. I stood up and quickly walked to the side of the chapel. Everyone saw me because no movement is allowed during count. The women broke out in laughter. Even the officer laughed. It was God's icebreaker. I knew the women were thinking, *I can relate to her*.

The count ended and I walked to the lectern laughing. The women laughed too. And that was just the beginning of their relating to me. I usually start by telling my own story, which—believe it or not—is so similar to theirs.

"Our forty-acre farm in the rolling hills of western Pennsylvania hardly looked like a prison," I began.

I continued to describe how the peaceful surroundings struck a sharp contrast to the reality of my life. My father was an angry, abusive alcoholic, but I loved him. He met my mother in a bar. She was a tiny, dark-haired spitfire of a woman who was grieving her recent divorce from her high-school sweetheart. Things progressed fast between them. As their relationship developed, my dad told her he was unable to have children. That was the *first* lie he told her.

My mother was furious when she became pregnant with me. She already had a son, Larry, from her first marriage, living with her mother. She didn't want to get married again, and she certainly didn't want to have a baby. My dad talked her into marriage, but her anger remained. I always felt it was focused at me, even before I knew their story.

Throughout my childhood I felt that surely my mother must be my stepmother. I daydreamed that one day a loving woman would appear at our front door to reclaim me. My imaginary mother would hug me and love me as I imagined a daughter should be loved. From very early on I was on a quest for love. My mom and dad soon discovered that a home built on deceit, unforgiveness, alcohol, and anger is a type of entrapment, a prison stronger than one surrounded by steel bars.

One November night in 1954 when I was in sixth grade, my dad came home from work on the railroad, and he was drunk, as he often was. From my bedroom window upstairs I always watched to see how he got out of the car. If he didn't stagger, I knew he was only half drunk, and then the night might go well. But if he staggered, I knew it was going to be another long night.

That night he started to fall as he got out of the car. I shuddered. I heard my mother yell at him as he entered the house. She had a way of agitating him, almost as if she wanted a battle. I often wondered why she didn't just let him go to bed and sleep it off.

Dinner began with a shout. "There's too much salt in these potatoes!" Dad yelled. He stood up, banged the chair back from the table, grabbed the dish of potatoes, and threw it out the back door. Mom threw something back at him.

Dad opened the cupboard door and began smashing

the dishes on the floor. I begged him to stop. Sometimes I could reason my dad down from one of these explosions. But not tonight. I didn't care about the dishes. I was afraid they were going to kill each other. Soon splintered glass was everywhere.

I tried to step between them. Dad shoved me aside, pushing me against the wall so hard I fell to the floor. This had happened before, more nights than I could count. And I was always scared. I got back up. *I can't take one more minute of this screaming and fighting,* I thought. I ran to the closet where Dad stored the shotgun he used for hunting. Grabbing the gun, I ran back to the kitchen. "I'm going to kill us all!" I screamed.

Dad immediately twisted the gun out of my hands and took it back to the closet. This bought me time. While he was putting it away, my mother and I escaped out the back door into the pine trees.

Soon we heard twigs snapping as he stumbled through the bushes in the back yard. We stood like statues, as still as possible so we wouldn't be found. And we were cold, so very cold, since we had had no time to get coats to protect us against the November chill. I remember thinking, *I have a spelling test tomorrow and I am not going to know my spelling words.*

As I stood trembling, frightened beyond reason, I heard him approach. I squeezed my eyes shut, silently praying, begging God for help. I was so terrified of what would happen if he found us that even the sound of my breath frightened me.

After a while, it became quiet. He had obviously gone back inside. From experience I knew that soon he would fall into a drunken sleep and we could sneak safely back inside. I don't remember going back into the house that night. I do remember that we had been outside for what seemed like an eternity. Once I got into bed I lay still, frightened and stiff, wondering if what felt like a nightmare was going to start over again.

My mother's resentment of my father spilled over into my life. As a young teenager I had promised myself that as soon as I found an escape route I'd get away from home. Consequently, I married the first time at seventeen, had a son, and then divorced at nineteen. That's when I decided to leave Pennsylvania. I remember thinking, *Maybe moving away from my family, hometown, and memories will make me a different person.*

I left in 1962 with one large black trunk and what seemed like a destroyed life. The invisible load of emotional baggage weighed far more than the trunk I dragged to the airport. Soon after arriving in Minneapolis, I met my husband, Dallas. He's six feet four—tall, handsome, and with a wonderful sense of humor. Everyone calls him Big D. One weekend his parents were out of town and I went to a party he was giving in their home. He became infatuated with me and wanted to see me every day. I enjoyed his attention.

Eventually I built up the courage to share my past with him. I told him that my dad was an alcoholic and my mother was also drinking heavily. I explained how they had each had affairs and were now divorced. Finally I said that I had been married and divorced, and had a little boy named Terry living back in Pennsylvania.

It took Dallas a few days to recover. However, when I

told him about my past, I'd also told him I would never get married again. That's what finally got him. He loved a challenge. After six months of turbulent dating, he asked, "Why don't we do this for the rest of our lives?"

We were married in April 1963. Within three months, I felt absolutely hopeless. I desperately missed my little boy and lived for my weekly talks with him. At the same time, I was devastated after each phone call and cried for the rest of the evening. Dallas didn't have a clue how to comfort me. Our schedules left little time for communicating anyway. I worked nights as a ticket agent for Northwest Airlines; he worked days as a material control analyst for Honeywell. We thought, *If we get away, we can get our marriage together,* so we went to Glacier Park in Montana. We fought as well in Glacier Park as we did in Minneapolis, Minnesota.

On a beautiful summer afternoon in June, 1963, Dallas had agreed to a ride in the country after lunch. I looked forward to time with him in the car because it was one place he couldn't get away from me. I was like a volcano, ready to erupt. Meaningful conversation between us was almost nonexistent.

Our lunch was in the oven when the phone rang. His baseball buddies were having a tournament and they were just one short. Would he join them? Just by hearing his side of the conversation I could tell he was going. I watched as he combed his hair and put on his new brown suede jacket. I was taking baked beans from the oven as he walked toward the back door, sarcastically whistling "You Are My Sunshine."

His teasing put me over the edge. I thought, *He's get-*

ting these beans one way or the other. I hurled the blue Corning Ware dish filled with hot beans.

I don't know who was more surprised when the beans found their mark. But he didn't say a word. He calmly wiped the beans off his jacket, opened the door, and walked out. He had threatened to leave me many times before, and this time I was afraid he was gone for good.

As I headed back to the kitchen, I remembered my parents' violence and realized I was following in their footsteps. I collapsed in tears and cried until I was exhausted. Taking a dishrag from the sink and wiping beans off the floor, I cried, "God, if there is a God, You've got to help me because I'm desperate. I can't make it one more day."

After I finished cleaning the kitchen, for some reason I didn't understand at that time, I began searching for the little white Bible Dallas had given me on our wedding day. *Where should I start reading?* I didn't know, so I started in Genesis and read the story of Adam and Eve. I remember thinking, *They had as many problems as we do,* and then I put the Bible back on the shelf.

Bored and lonely, I searched for something to do. On any other night, after any other fight, I would have escaped to join my friends. The women at work always knew where to find a party and I was a regular at most of them. I'd been running away from fights all my life. That night, though, something kept me home. (I learned later that my in-laws, Howard and Florence Strom, were fasting and praying for us.)

I tried to find something to get my mind off the fight. I felt abandoned and frightened about our situation. I picked up the newspaper and read in the TV section that Billy Graham was speaking about marriage that night. Desperate for answers on that subject, I turned on the television.

I don't remember too much of what he said about marriage, but Graham seemed to be speaking directly to me, almost as if he knew all about my life. One verse that he mentioned particularly grabbed my attention: "As many as received Him [Jesus], to them He gave power to become children of God (John 1:12, TLB)."

Power? I certainly didn't know anything about power. All my life I had felt powerless and weak. I hadn't been able to change my circumstances or myself. I had tried, over and over. Could God really give me power to change? Could my life be different?

Besides feeling powerless all my life, I longed for someone to love me unconditionally. Billy Graham had said I could insert myself in John 3:16, so I opened the Bible and fumbled through the pages until I found the book of John. Then I read the verse aloud, "For God so loved Linda that He gave His one and only begotten Son, that if she believes in Him, she could have everlasting life."

"God, is that true?" I whispered. "Do you really love me? Please love me." For the first time in my life I felt immersed in love.

When Dallas finally came home several days later, I was happy to see him and tried to explain what had happened. He looked down at me and hesitantly said, "It should be a lot safer around here if what you say is true."

Over the next several months, Dallas saw me gradually change. On a trip to visit his family in Iowa, we drove to Omaha, Nebraska, to hear Billy Graham speak. As we drove home, without saying anything to me at the time, he quietly invited Jesus into his own life. Several months later my son Terry came to live with us. We began to establish our own family, leaning on the grace of God to help us break out of the destructive patterns we had known for so long.

I spoke Friday night and Saturday morning at Mountain View Prison. As I finished my story, I was again overwhelmed by how faithful God had been to me. I loved the message Christ was preaching to me *through me*. I could see the inmates' surprise as I spoke. Here I was, a middle-aged suburban housewife. I looked average, normal. Yet our stories were so, so similar. The women seemed to relax a bit. They realized we were on level ground. Like them, I was in the process of healing. I just happened to live outside the walls.

But that was enough of my talking. It was time for them to look at their own lives. I told them, "We will break into groups of six or so to discuss some of what you've just heard—how it applies to your life—and to have an opportunity to get to know one another better. Each group will include volunteers and inmates."

As they began forming small groups, a young woman approached me. I asked her name. With tears in her eyes she told me, "My name's Denise. I really need to find God. I have an incurable disease." I talked with her for a few moments about Jesus' love for her. I believe that touching people when they are at a point of need can be a blessing, but usually I ask before I hug someone. So I said, "Denise, I'd like to hug you."

She closed her eyes, lowered her face, looked at the floor, and mumbled, "I have AIDS."

"Oh, Denise," I said, "I'm so sorry," and for several minutes I held her in my arms as she wept.

I motioned to a pew close by so we could talk. She told me our lives were similar. She too had been beaten by men. She added that her story included becoming a prostitute and a drug addict. She was not sure how she contracted AIDS, but she knew she was destined to go to hell. As I heard her story, I thought, *She's already gone through hell.* I could feel her shaking as I held her tighter.

I withdrew my arms so I could sit back and look directly at her. "Denise, I know it's not an accident that we're together right now. God's brought us together and He really loves you." I paused and continued to look into her eyes.

I took her hands in mine. I could still feel her shaking. "I, too, have felt fearful," I said. "Can I pray for you, that God's love will get rid of the fear? There is a Bible verse that says, 'Perfect love drives out fear (1 John 4:18).' That means God's love gets rid of your fear. I know it's hard to trust. It was hard for me to trust too. But I can tell you from my own life that Jesus is true to His word."

I began to pray, asking God to do for her what He did for me, what He longs to do for anyone willing to ask: "Lord, Denise's heart is open, please touch her right now."

As I prayed for Denise and the other women-in-white, I thought, *God, I need to trust You myself. These women are going back into the prison population where they are known by a number rather than a name, where there is no privacy or place to be still, where there is fighting and rape, and where anger is the one acceptable emotion. So hard to trust. Help me to put them in Your hands.*

As the seminar drew to a close on Sunday, I looked at the inmates standing in the middle aisle or alongside the chapel walls, or coming to kneel at the altar. I thought about the stories I'd heard during moments of prayer throughout the weekend and the pain and sorrow of broken homes, broken promises, broken lives.

Wiping tears from my eyes, I ended the service Sunday morning by telling the women about my grandmother. "Being with her during the summer months was the highlight of my year," I said. "She always told me, 'God is greater than anything you will face.' And I saw my grandmother praying for me. She lived in Randolph, New York, and it was always hard for her to send me back home because I had told her what was going on with my parents. As I left she would always assure me, 'I will pray for you every day, as long as I live.'"

I asked the women, "How many of you have someone praying for you today? Or know of someone who has prayed for you?"

About half of the women raised their hands.

"Today you are being prayed for. People are praying all

during these weekends for you to experience the God who loves you and knows you by name." *There is hope for me,* their eyes seemed to say.

"My grandma and I used to walk together every night right after dinner. We would buy an Eskimo Pie for ten cents at the gas station, and head off down the old swamp road. As we walked, she would tell me about heaven and her friend Jesus.

"But no matter what we were talking about, she'd stop at a certain tree and we'd have to turn around and head back home. Each night I would hope that she'd forget that tree was there and we could walk forever. Those walks were my happiest childhood memories.

"A few years ago I took Dallas back to the old swamp road so we could take my favorite journey together. As we started down the road, I was amazed. 'Where is the beauty I saw as a child?' I asked. 'This is nothing but a swamp.' I wondered why I hadn't noticed this back then.

"Those childhood walks weren't wonderful because the road was beautiful. As a child enjoying long walks on a summer's evening, I never looked at the swamp or at the road. I was too busy looking into my grandmother's eyes.

"It's the same for you this morning," I told the women. "You're walking on the old swamp road. But it doesn't matter what the road is like, it's who you're walking with."

❖ ❖ ❖

Earlier that weekend, as guards had cleared Rosalie and me to leave the prison, Chaplain Crosby had asked,

"Would you like to go to Death Row after you finish in the chapel tomorrow?"

My heart raced. I had wanted to go to Death Row, but knowing how difficult it was to get clearance, I'd put it out of my mind. "Absolutely," I quickly replied. "I was hoping you'd ask."

Although we were exhausted that evening when we returned to our motel room, sleep was hard to come by. *How will I relate to these women living with a death sentence?* I wondered apprehensively. *Maybe I'll just sit there and cry.* I had no idea what crimes they had committed but I imagined the women were frightened, sad, and lonely. Then I prayed and meditated on Scripture. In the book of Hebrews, God promises to never leave us or forsake us. Never. As I fell asleep, the word picture I was to share became clear: this promise, this assurance, was God's message to those women.

I remembered that promise after the service on Sunday as Chaplain Crosby led us from the red brick chapel to the small, fenced-in area just a few short steps away, known as Death Row. "Love through me, Father," I prayed. I felt totally unprepared for what I was about to experience. As we drew closer Chaplain Crosby casually commented, "As you can tell after this weekend, Linda, things can get pretty overwhelming around here. Sometimes I get discouraged and feel I need a place of refuge. That's why I come to Death Row several times each week. The women pray for me, and I always leave encouraged."

Death Row is a prison within a prison, separated from the rest of the compound by a shorter six-foot fence.

That year, Death Row inmates worked six hours a day inside a separate, mesh-enclosed work-room creating Parole Pals: large stuffed girl and boy dolls with dimpled knees and faces. The demand was so great for these Cabbage Patch-type dolls that only prison officials had the opportunity to custom-order them.

Outside the work area, a small day room was decorated with crocheted tablecloths and throws tossed over park-like benches securely bolted to the gray cement floor. A television set and bookshelves, filled with well-worn hardcover and paperback books and magazines, stood against the outside wall, under the window. The women were free to walk about these rooms during the day. At 10:30 P.M. on weeknights and 1:30 A.M. on weekends they were locked into their individual barred cells.

Two women, Karla Faye Tucker and Pamela Perillo, were watching for me. I saw them waving excitedly behind the small, mesh window in the steel door. Bouncing up and down, Karla was enthusiastically signing "I love you" as she waved. I was amazed at how pretty and joy-filled she was.

When I walked through the door, I was warmly welcomed. Karla said, "During the sessions on Friday and Saturday Chaplain Crosby gave us reports about how things were going in the chapel. We could hear the women singing through the open windows."

From the beginning, Karla demonstrated an unchanging quality. She wasn't self-focused; she focused on what God was doing around her. Our first conversation centered on what had happened in the general prison population that weekend. I was astounded. This wasn't at all what I had expected and my apprehension quickly disappeared. I thought I was going into Death Row to encourage and comfort. Instead, I quickly understood why Chaplain Crosby loved to come here.

Karla sat down between Chaplain Crosby and me. A barrette struggled to keep her long brown hair in place, but strands of curls escaped and framed her face. She turned to me and smiled. "Chap says you have a story that really touches the women," she said. "We can't wait to hear it. Tell us about it."

I took a deep breath and began to tell them about my spiritual journey. After a while I paused and looked into their faces. I could tell they related to the pain in my life as they empathized with my story. Then it hit me. In the direction I had been heading, I, too, could have been on Death Row.

We laughed and cried together as we exchanged stories. I was amazed at how at home I felt in the white, cement-block room. Time flew by as it had in the chapel. Dressed in white, Karla and Pam knelt down beside me, laid their hands on me, and prayed, "Lord, thank You for bringing Linda here today. Continue to open doors for her. Refresh her now as she heads back to Milwaukee. And bring her back to us again."

Before leaving, I remembered the assurance the Lord gave me the night before, and I shared one last story.

"When I was growing up, Susan was my closest friend. She lived near Pymatuning Lake, the largest man-made lake in Pennsylvania. We would sit on her boat dock, our feet dangling in the water, and talk for hours. I lived what seemed like miles away from her, up a long dirt road. When I had to go home, she usually walked with me, but only as far as the dirt road. Then we would say good-bye and she would head back to her house. I was left to walk alone the rest of the way.

"There was only one house between the lake road and my home. A forest lined both sides of the uneven road. Sometimes I was afraid of the unknown. How could I know what kind of danger waited for me behind every curve or over the next hill? Usually I just dreaded the known, what I would face at home. My stomach was in knots as I peered through the pine trees to see if my dad's car was in the driveway."

I told Karla and Pam, "I was so thankful Chaplain Crosby said I could come to Death Row. Last night as I was praying for you, I remembered how afraid I was as a little girl on that walk home. I never knew what frightening experience was ahead. I felt alone then. And I thought about you, and what you must be feeling, facing unknown dangers on your walk. Jesus told me to tell you, 'When you get to the dirt road, I'm walking all the way home with you.'" It was a still, quiet moment. God was present and it was holy.

We hugged each other and said good-bye. The door clanged shut behind me. Sensing I needed some time alone, Chaplain Crosby escorted me to his office in the chapel and closed the door. As he left, I sat down, laid my head on his desk, and wept. I realized I was hooked. I knew that if God allowed, I would be back.

Chapter Three

Amazing Grace

Therefore, I tell you, her many sins have been forgiven—for she loved much. But he who has been forgiven little loves little.

—Luke 7:47

When I was forgiven and experienced forgiveness, it freed me inside to soar. I went higher and deeper with the Lord. When we hold unforgiveness we block communication and intimacy. Forgiveness is not based on how we feel, because if it was we would never forgive. Forgiveness is based on a command by God—"Forgive us our trespasses as we forgive those who trespass against us."

—Karla Faye Tucker

When I first visited Death Row, peace was evident. But it was Karla's joy that was surprising. That joy led me to bring hundreds of people over many years to this place she called Life Row. As she said, "The Life of the Lord is here!"

In 1988, Dallas joined me in Gatesville. Over the next three years, I began sharing Mountain View stories at my weekly Bible study in Milwaukee. I displayed a photo of

Top: Karla being escorted by a guard through the prison. Even in handcuffs, Karla's joy was radiant.
Bottom: The gatehouse at the Mountain View Unit. Staff and volunteers enter through the door on the left. Inmates being transported go through the gate on right.

the Death Row women as a reminder to pray for them. I read their letters and referred to events in their lives in our monthly newsletters. Each year, our ministry team grew.

Between visits, I corresponded with both Karla and Pam. In a letter, Pam described how they met in 1983, before Karla was a Christian, when Pam was brought from Death Row in Gatesville to Houston on a bench warrant. Karla was waiting to be sentenced. Pam wrote,

> I was brought [to Harris County Jail in Houston]
> for a legal issue related to my case. Believing that
> Karla would most likely receive the death penalty,
> someone arranged for us to meet. One day while I was
> in the exercise area a guard brought her to me.
> Knowing Karla now it's difficult to believe, but then
> she had no expression on her face or in her eyes. She
> looked blank and hard. It was the same cold, dark look
> that I'd seen on the television reports. But I could tell
> she was scared. I described Death Row and what it's
> like to be here, imprisoned twenty-four hours a day,
> with only one five-minute telephone call permitted
> every ninety days.

By the time she came to live with Pam on Death Row in Gatesville, Karla had given her life to Christ. Pam's own faith continued to develop over the years as she and Karla shared their struggles and encouragements with one another.

The friendship between the two women was strong when I met them. Like all friends, Karla, Pam, and I began to share our everyday lives. For example, in one letter Karla wrote,

> Everything is going good here. He continues to bless me daily, in the hard times as well as the easy ones. God has burdened my heart with learning how to use sign language as a ministry tool, and it is going great. When y'all are here next time, we will do a song for you. And guess what? Frances Newton, a new sister on the Row, will join us!

✦ ✦ ✦

When our ministry team returned in 1990, our fourth year of ministry at Mountain View, Chaplain Crosby asked us to come early and spend Wednesday through Friday on Death Row. The weekend seminar for the general population would begin Friday night.

We prayed and then opened our session on Wednesday with Luke 7:47: "Therefore, I tell you, her many sins have been forgiven—for she loved much. But he who has been forgiven little loves little." I looked around at the small group and said, "Lord, it's so true. We do love you, and all of us have been forgiven so much."

Karla nodded as if the words were written about her. She then began telling her incredible account of receiving forgiveness in the corner of her Harris County Jail cell.

"I was awaiting my trial when a prison ministry group visited the jail. I just went to see what it was like. They were putting on a puppet show. When I walked through the door, my mouth kind of dropped. I felt something that I had never felt before. I know now that it was the presence of God. I remember looking at the ministry team and I don't know how I knew they had been where I was at, but inside I knew they had been in jails and prisons, been into prostitution, violence, and drugs. I remember thinking, *I want to feel what they're feeling.* They had a peace and a joy—something that was real. I had never seen that in anybody.

"That night when the service was over I snuck a Bible. I wasn't aware that they gave Bibles out freely to help people in jail, so I thought I was stealing it. I took it with me to my cell and hid back in the corner.

"I opened the Bible and started reading. I don't know how long it took, but I remember that I was kneeling on the floor, crying, asking God to come into my heart and forgive me for what I had done.

"I don't know that I felt forgiven at that point, but I do know I felt love. I knew that no matter what I had done I was loved, just like that, just like I was. That's when the whole weight of what I did fell on me. I realized for the first time that I had brutally murdered two people and there were people out there hurting because of me. Yet God was saying, 'I love you.' It was supernatural. I don't really know how to explain it. At that moment, He reached down inside of me and ripped out that violence at the very roots and poured Himself in.

"I knew then that I had to tell the truth about everything. Before I knew the Lord, I didn't care what anybody else felt or thought. I didn't want to tell what had happened for fear of what the consequences would be.

When the Lord came into my life and changed me, I realized I couldn't count the cost of my own life. I had to tell the truth about everything.

"I was not fearful of what man could do to me. Instead I was fearful of what God could do to me if I didn't tell the truth. That is far more serious because we are dealing with eternity. After that night in the Harris County Jail I was set free. God is so real. He is awesome.

"Just recently some relationship issues surfaced. A friend confronted me. 'Karla,' she said, 'You're angry at your mother!' At first I denied it, but then I wondered, 'Where were you, Mother?' Our household was crazy. I began using marijuana with my sisters when I was seven or eight years old and heroin by the time I was ten. When my parents finally divorced, I opted to live with my mother. I idolized her. I wanted to be just like her. Yet the things she did confused me.

"When I was fourteen she began to school me in the art of being a call girl. I wanted to please her so much. I wanted her to be proud of me. So instead of saying no, I just tried to do what she asked. But deep down inside I knew that what I was doing was wrong.

"I also noticed the difference between my sisters and me. I never felt like I was a part of my family. Maybe it was because I was so dark, with brown hair and dark eyes. My sisters were very, very blonde, with blue eyes and fair skin. People teased me about it. It got inside of me and made me wonder, *Do I belong here?*

"One day my mother told me that I was the result of an affair. She seemed happy about it and acted as if I should be, too. As a young girl I didn't know how to articulate what I was going through. I didn't know how to come to my mom and say, 'You cheated on my dad and I'm the result and that hurts me. Help me handle this. Help me deal with the feeling of being disconnected from everyone.'"

With that, Karla paused, her eyes brimmed with tears, "My mother died on Christmas Eve in 1979 and it still hurts. I never got to ask her all the 'whys,' and I'm not sure she would have had any answers that would have helped if I had. Now I finally realize that I'm angry with her and need prayer. I want to forgive her."

We sat quietly for a minute before everyone got up and gathered around her. Words are inadequate at moments like these, but the Lord promises to always receive us. I knelt beside Karla and whispered, "Though my father and mother forsake me, the LORD will lift me up," quoting Psalm 27:10. "Lift up your hands, Karla, like a little child. Let the Lord pick you up and hold you safely in His arms. He heals the brokenhearted. His healing love will enable you to forgive."

As our time of prayer was ending, Chaplain Crosby arrived to escort us back to the main gate. He quietly joined our circle. As their pastor, he extended his hands over us and recited the benediction from the book of Jude: "To him who is able to keep you from falling and to present you before his glorious presence without fault and with great joy—to the only God our Savior be glory, majesty, power and authority, through Jesus Christ our Lord."

Years later in June of 1993, Karla wrote a poem about the night she took that Bible back to her prison cell:

The Lord's Show

It seems like so many years ago that I went to see
    this show.
There were puppets
    and people who used to be just like me
But they were really different, these people.
This I would soon be able to see.
As I entered the room with them
My body felt weird
All through each limb.
I walked to a chair, and then I sat down
My mouth wide open, hanging almost to the
    ground.
Then I heard a cackle from a girl named Ellen
What's going on? I wondered,
But there was just no tellin'.
That was the last sound I remember hearing
At the show that night
But I remember seeing people
They glowed with such a wonderful light!
The message I heard, but not by their words
For God's presence was there,
YES! It was everywhere!
Their faces all glowed
As the Holy Ghost flowed
Jesus delivered me that night from death to LIFE
    ROW!
I went to that show with wrong intentions, I must
    confess.
But when I left that night I could hardly walk, I
    was so blessed.

I snuck a Bible back to my cell
For something was happening
But what I still couldn't tell!
I sat on my bunk
And in the corner I sunk.
You see, I needed to hide
For I was still so full of pride.
But as I opened that Book and started to read
Pretty soon I was on the floor
Down on my knees
I asked for forgiveness as the tears did fall
"Come into my heart Lord Jesus, I'll give you my
    all.
"O God I'm begging You, please set me free
Come into my life and give me liberty.
You said You love me,
But I just can't see
How such a lost sinner
Can ever be a winner."
Then Jesus put His arms around me
And gently said,
"My precious child, your sins are forgiven;
    you are no longer dead."
The puddle beneath me was quite a sight,
I was redeemed by the blood of the Lamb that
    night.
As I looked at my tears in the puddle below,
I thanked my Savior for that awesome show.
And then all of a sudden I knew without a doubt
The Holy Ghost had come with a mighty shout
He opened my eyes and to my surprise

I was given new life
He made me His wife!
Yes, I remember that night so long ago.
I remember it well, Jesus.
It was quite a show!

❖ ❖ ❖

The next afternoon we saw three faces pressed against the small window as we entered the compound: Karla, Pam, and Frances Newton, whom we had met the night before. The guard unlocked the door and like an excited child at Christmas Karla said, "We have a surprise for you."

We sat down on one of the benches as Pam took a cassette tape and walked over to the tape player, joining Frances and Karla already standing in front of the mesh-enclosed window. "Amazing Grace" began to fill the room. The words pierced my soul. Thoughts of Karla's story were still fresh in my mind. Three women—condemned by the world, yet redeemed by God—passionately began to sign with their hands the words to the age-less hymn. We silently joined their chorus of gratitude. (As Karla often said, "We all had 'God bumps.'")

That day we talked about forgiveness again, beginning by reading Ephesians 4:32: "Be kind and compassionate to one another, forgiving each other, just as in Christ God forgave you." I told the women some of my own thoughts on the power of forgiveness.

I explained that I used to live near Lake Michigan. One day as I was driving I saw a house being moved forward. I stopped and saw why. The lake's pounding waves had eroded the shoreline. If they didn't move the house forward, it would be destroyed. It would crash into the lake.

Allowing unforgiveness to remain in our hearts is like ignoring the erosion. Our hearts become eroded and if we don't forgive, if we don't move forward, our lives are destroyed. Forgiveness is not denying, ignoring or forgetting what we experienced or how we feel. In spite of our best efforts to forget what we've done to others or what others have done to us, we can't forget the past. Our minds are greater than any computer and have an excellent, but usually unforgiving, memory.

There are two ways, however, to remember an event. One is by reliving it, allowing the pain, anger, fear, or bitterness to consume or control us. We can even become self-righteous toward others as we harbor the wounds. The other way of remembering is to allow God's process of forgiveness to be activated in our lives. Painful events are a fact of history. They happened, but they no longer control us.

Forgiveness is a process. I have grieved what might have been. There was a time when my mother's behavior controlled me. A phone call could destroy my whole day. Each time these things surfaced, Dallas and I prayed together for God's grace and for me to be free of the pain. In obedience to Christ, I forgave my mother. We've learned that both healing and forgiveness come from the hand of God, and my mom has been released in the process."

At one point when I was sharing some of my experience with forgiveness, Karla looked at the group and said, "Forgiveness is so powerful. It reminds me of what happened in my life because of Peggy Kurtz. Peggy is the sister of Jerry Dean, one of my victims. Back when I committed my crime, and no one knew who did it, she went to church. When she walked in, her whole congregation began to pray for the salvation of the person who killed her brother. Yes! I know the angels in heaven were shouting praises to the Lord as He smiled and knew right then that another lost soul would be won to Him. She prayed for that person—me—from day one. Those prayers are what moved God's hand in my life. I know that just as sure as I am sitting here.

"Right after I got the death penalty and was still just a babe in my spiritual diapers, I got a note from her saying she forgave me and loved me, and Jesus forgave me and loves me. She asked if I would call her so we could talk. After about a week or two I finally called. It was awesome. That conversation grounded me in my love for Christ. I knew then that I would never turn from the Lord. I knew He would always be my life."

When Karla said those words, I didn't know many details of her crime or specifics about Peggy's forgiveness. It wasn't until years later, after Karla's death, that I called Peggy and asked if she would share her story.

✦ ✦ ✦

Early one Saturday morning, my friend Donna Dixon and I sat across a table from Peggy in a Houston restaurant. I learned why this woman had such an impact on Karla's life and faith.

"I can't tell you how difficult this is," Peggy began, crying softly. "So you'll have to forgive my tears. I got saved in August 1982. My husband, Fred, was vice president of a large national company, and we had every material possession we could possibly want. But he was on his way to becoming an alcoholic, and I was an unfaithful wife. We had gone just about as far as we could go in the other direction." Peggy paused. "I hate sin. It destroys people. It tears families apart.

"My husband's company had a warehouse full of goods that they wanted to give away as a tax write-off. Fred came home one day and said, 'Peggy, I met a man I want you to meet. His name is John Counts and he wants us to come to his church.'

"I said, 'Fred, I'm not into that. You go ahead.'

"He said, 'No. I met with him for breakfast and we made arrangements to donate everything. This man wants us to come to his church so they can thank us. Just come and be with me.'

"That Sunday we walked into Living Word Outreach. Everybody was clapping and praising the Lord; they looked like a wild bunch of people. No one talked to me about the love of Jesus, but I just somehow knew it was there. I started clapping my hands and singing praises like I'd been there forever. These people had something I didn't have. I think salvation started the minute I walked in the door.

"On the drive home Fred said, 'What did you think?' and I said, 'I don't know but I want to go back.' I was never the same person after that. I don't think anyone led me to the Lord. I just knew who He was.

"My brother-in-law was dying of cancer and like any

other new Christian I said, 'All we've gotta do is pray; God will heal him.' I believed Him. I knew He would never lie to me. I knew I could trust Him. When my brother-in-law died, I was devastated. I thought, 'Wait a minute, I have to rethink this. He died and I believed that he'd be healed. What happened?' It was through that experience of learning to trust Him in spite of how things go that God did a deep work in my heart, preparing me for what was ahead with my brother.

"Jerry was my buddy. He was eleven years younger than I was. He had lived with my husband and me in Sugarland, Texas, when he got out of the Coast Guard. We went to the movies and out to eat together. We had such good times.

"My dad wanted him to come back to Alabama because mom had a stroke, but Jerry knew that opportunity lay in Houston. He had a really good job with a security company, they were talking about putting in a computer room, and—"

Peggy stopped, crying harder. Bowing her head, she prayed, "I am healed, I am healed."

She began again. "As we traveled to Alabama to celebrate Christmas with our parents, Jerry excitedly told us he was in line for a manager's position. He also talked about Shawn, a woman he was dating, and mentioned an encounter with her friend, Karla. He told me, 'Man, I've never met a woman like her before. You say anything cross to her and she'll just hit you.' His glasses were broken. Karla had hit him. I told him, 'Jerry, stay away from her. If a woman is that violent, you don't need to be around her.' That was the first time I heard her name.

"I saw Jerry again in January 1983. He told me that he was thinking about marrying Shawn, but Daddy was totally against it. I tried to talk him out of it, too. I said, 'Jerry, your life is in a turmoil and you need Jesus. You'll never know until you receive Him what healing, what peace He brings.'

"He replied, 'You know, Peggy girl, there's something different about you. I was going to tell you and Fred on the way to Alabama that I have noticed a real change in you.'

"'Jerry, you can have that change.'

"He said, 'Well, I'm not ready yet. But I'm going to think about it.'

"So I guess he got married. I called him in March and he said it wasn't working out, that she had a bad temper too. I tried to witness to him more—you just never know what God's doing in a person's heart. If I could have known that this was the last time we'd talk, I'd have talked more about Christ.

"Father's Day was coming up and I hadn't heard from him. I called his work and they told me he had been killed. I said, 'I think you've got the wrong person.' Nobody's ever prepared. I thought maybe he had been killed in a car accident or on the job. They said, 'No, he was murdered.' I guess I passed out. My supervisor called our pastor. He came over and helped me. Somehow I got home that day.

"But then everything started: newspapers, TV, radio. My parents had to come from Alabama. I've never, never seen two people as devastated as they were. Mama broke down at the funeral home; it was all Dad could do to stand. I guess what hurts more than anything else is what that type of death does to a family. It comes in and rips you apart.

"Week after week went by. With all the news media and everybody talking about the murder, I had nightmares almost every night. I'd see the walls covered in blood and I didn't know how to get out. I'd wake up screaming.

"I knew that if I heard one more thing about this murder I was going to go through the roof. One morning Fred said, 'Peggy, you've got to get a handle on your life. You're letting this thing take control of you.' And on the way to work, I was praying. I asked God to relieve me from this ball and chain. Wednesday night, July 18, 1983, I went to church. The minute I walked in, Pastor John said, 'Peggy, come down front, we want to pray for you.' As people gathered around me he instructed, 'Just lift up your hands, put all your anger, all your bitterness, all the bad dreams in them. Then give everything up to the Lord.'

"I was so ready. I couldn't work; I couldn't sleep; I couldn't eat. I couldn't escape it. It was constantly on my mind. I was literally filling my mind with the Word of God. I was eating it for breakfast. I was eating it for supper. I knew the answer was in the Word, but I couldn't figure out how to apply it.

"So as my church family stood with me, I prayed, 'God, make a way for me. I forgive whoever did this. I don't want to go backward in my walk, I want to go forward. You said to forgive. Your Word says I'm supposed to cast everything on You. You've helped other people; help me.'

"There is power in a praying church. Karla and Danny were apprehended that night, thirty-five days after Jerry's murder. The next morning I discovered they were arrested. But I had no sooner given it up to the Lord, and my anger started all over again. Now there were faces. Finally I had someone to put my hatred on. I had from Thursday to Sunday to hate. Then I said, 'No, I am not going to do this. God has set me free and what God has freed is free indeed.' I'm still free."

Peggy gulped back fresh tears. "I loved that boy. I loved him so much. Sunday morning as I sat in church, I realized there was a battle going on in my mind. I wondered what brought Karla to the point of taking another person's life. What hatred and bitterness must have been in her—Jerry could have been me, he could have been anybody that got in her way at that time. Every time I saw something on TV, it triggered a memory of what took place.

"I didn't want to be consumed by hate. So, I told the Lord that now that I had a face to put to the crime, I still chose to forgive, and that if He made it possible, I'd tell Karla. I was set free that day. I came out of the prison that I'd been in. I knew that the devil lost that round. God allowed me to struggle during those thirty-five days. I knew all too well that if we hate someone, we're right there with them, bound by our hatred. I wanted my mind and my heart to be filled with the Word of God. I had to take every thought captive. It's obedience to Christ. I could not let my mind become absorbed with the details of the crime. Instead I began praying every day for their salvation. I knew God could change them.

"A man at our church was in prison ministry and several months later told me about the reports of Karla's conversion. He said that if I wanted to talk to her, he would arrange it. I couldn't call her, they would not allow that. She had to call me. I just went limp. I didn't know where to put my thoughts. I didn't know how to 'take every thought captive.' I didn't know what to do. All day long I paced and cried out, 'What do I say, Lord? You've just got to help me. You've just got to, Lord.' And He said, 'Remember your commitment. Remember your promise.' And I said, 'Yes, Lord.'

"And that got me through. We owned our own business and Karla was going to call us there. When the phone rang, I tried not to think of anything but God. I said, 'Karla, I forgive you. I told the Lord that if He made it possible, I'd tell you I forgive you.'

"She said, 'Thank you, Peggy. I wanted so much to be able to tell at least one of the family members that I'm sorry.'

"It's like it happened yesterday. I don't think we ever get rid of the pain to the extent that we don't cry, but the Lord showed me something important about what had just happened. You know where the Bible says we are to 'lay up treasures in heaven'? We usually hear those verses used in reference to giving money to God's work. But the Lord showed me that *forgiveness* is a treasure! So being able to forgive in spite of this hurt in my heart is something He calls a treasure. It's His treasure of amazing grace.

"I keep needing to reaffirm my decision to forgive though. This thing would die down and be brought back up, die down and be brought back up. Newspapers and television interviews went over and over the crime. I remember one particularly difficult newspaper article that took me by surprise. I was upset by what I read and I wrote Karla a letter. I said it was like experiencing the wounds all over again. I told her she couldn't possibly know how much we loved Jerry and asked her not to say another negative word about him. It wasn't just for me, it was for my parents, for my brothers and sisters.

"I couldn't bear to work that day. I walked around the house saying, 'Wait a minute, God, I've forgiven her. Wait a minute. You told me that when Christ shed His blood on the cross, it covered everything.' But I was dealing with a gut feeling that I couldn't shake off. I knew He wanted me to come back to Him every time my emotions struck. He is the Judge and so I went to Him and said, 'Lord, now there's *this* offense.' But He said, 'No, Jesus covered it.'"

As Peggy paused, I knew exactly what she was talking about. I told her, "When details of the crime came out, Peggy, they really bothered Karla, too. Someone from the Texas Board of Pardons and Paroles came to the prison after she received her execution date. He questioned her about the reasons behind what she did. Instead of trying to excuse herself or blame anyone else, Karla told him, 'How can you make sense out of a senseless act?' That response cost her.

"In 1993 Karla wrote me a letter about you. When Karla wrote, she usually stayed very focused on our relationship and the Lord. This letter was one of the few times she referred to the crime or to the people involved.

But you were very important to her. Is it okay if I read part of it?"

Peggy nodded.

I picked up the letter and read,

> Please pray that any articles and interviews about my crime will not continue to hurt others. Several of them devastated my victims' families and mine—the people I have tried all these years to protect! They were hurt deeply. For the first time, Peggy Kurtz has agreed to do an interview for the *700 Club*. She's the incredible person I told you about who forgave me. Please pray for us. God could reach a lot of people with this interview. Even if He reaches just one, it will be worth it. I want all the glory to go to God.

Peggy said, "That interview was difficult, but I'm thankful I had the opportunity to share what God did in my life. My decision to forgive became my anchor, something I came back to time after time. Jesus said we're to forgive seventy times seven. Sometimes we need to do that with the same person. I hated the circumstances that took Jerry out of my life, but he is in the hands of the Lord. I didn't lose him. I know where he is. Karla became like a little sister to me."

Peggy had begun to gather her things, preparing to leave. But then she sank back in the booth. She whispered, "You know what I miss most? Karla's prayers. I know she prayed for me. How I miss them. I always wanted to get to know her. But other than our letters back and forth, the Lord seemed to say it wasn't the time. But I will get to know her, in heaven. Then we can share all we want and neither of us will have to feel any of the pain or shed any of the tears."

We hugged good-bye at the door, promising to talk soon. Donna and I watched Peggy leave and then began walking back to our hotel room. My mind was whirling: *Forgiveness—what a link it is in Your hands, God. Your amazing grace was extended to Peggy, and Peggy forgave Karla. Karla received Your forgiveness and so was able to receive Peggy's forgiveness. Then people came to the Row, one after another, and Your mercy changed their lives.*

Part II

Traveling Together

Top: Karla in prison.
Bottom: The decorated car that took Dana to Karla after the wedding.

Chapter Four

His Banner over Me Is Love

He has taken me to the banquet hall, and his banner over me is love.

—Song of Songs 2:4

I've not met another woman, another person, like Karla. From the moment I met her I could feel God's presence surrounding her. There are so many things I could say about her beauty and genuineness, but the most important thing for me is to make sure people know her heart's cry—for the body of Christ to be unified, to look past denominations, past race, past the prison wall, and be whole.

—Dana Brown, American Horizon,
September/October 1998

There's a future that I hope for and that I believe for with my husband. And still, ultimately, if I'm executed that's just a train ride home.

—Karla Faye Tucker

I teased Karla about writing epistles when she wrote letters. I needed a good half-hour to read one! I'd make a pot of hot tea, find a quiet spot, and picture her excitement as she'd bring me up-to-date on her life. That's what I did when I received a seven-page, single-spaced, typed letter that she had written on February 15, 1995. After I began reading, I realized how appropriate it was that she wrote it the day after Valentine's Day.

> Until '92 I still had a problem with men because of my past experiences. I didn't see it as a problem, but now I know it was. I never thought I would want to be married, especially being on Death Row. When I went to [Harris] County Jail in '92, to get my first [execution] date, God started dealing with my heart concerning men and Christian marriages.
>
> I would see couples like you and Dallas, with Christ as their center and foundation, and I never imagined it could happen for me. At least not as long as I was here. But I started feeling a tug on my heart. How wonderful it would be to have a husband cherish me like Paul instructed. Could it be the Lord's will for me to marry a sold-out, Holy Ghost–filled, on-fire-for-Jesus, godly man? The Lord would have to let me out of here for that to happen.
>
> Have you ever experienced God having completely different plans for you than you have for yourself???!! Yep, I thought you had. (Smile!) Well, when I got back from Harris County I got a wonderful little article about marriage. As I read it, I thought, *Yes, I want this, Lord. If*

You are going to let me out, then please be preparing my heart for my husband, even as I pray.

But my prayer was always with the stipulation that He was going to let me out of here. Well, just two days later I was doing an interview with Mike Barber's prison ministry. He and Dana Brown came walking through the door and I knew instantly that Dana was the man God had chosen for me!

I had known Dana since he started working for Mike, but I always felt just sisterly love toward him. I never even noticed how good-looking he was until that day! But boy, howdy, I sure noticed it then! I try not to question God, but you can be sure I questioned Him on this! After all, here I was on Life Row, not knowing if I would ever get out. *Why* should I get involved with someone and put all of us through this!?

I said, "God, if this is really You telling me that Dana is the man, then You are going to have to bring it about because I ain't helping You!!!" And to make this very long story as short as I can, I never told *anyone*. I kept quiet for over a year, still wondering if this was just me. With me being in here and Dana living in the free world, I didn't feel worthy of him. God had to deal with me on that, too.

About nineteen months later I got my confirmation!!! On November 18, 1993, (my birthday) I received a card from Dana. God had put me on his heart in a special, supernatural way and I knew right then that it was *God!* I came to find out that he had felt this way for over a year!!! Isn't God awesome?

After that, we began corresponding. He was advised to cut it off and see if this was really God. We stopped writing for almost two months. Then God brought us back together. He was advised again to really seek God. We fasted for twenty-four days on nothing but liquids, praying that the Lord would give us confirmation and trying to draw deeper into Him.

After those twenty-four days we got our word from the Lord!!! And it was the desire of our heart. We went forward in a serious relationship and shared it with everyone. Dana didn't know we would get married at this point, but I did. SMILE! So I tried not to get ahead of God and Dana, but to be patient and let God show him what He had already shown me. This was hard.

As time went on, the Lord knit our hearts together. In August 1994, Dana asked me to marry him. Now we are just waiting for the Lord to make a way because we don't want to do this by proxy. But we did sit in the visiting room and say our vows before the Lord. We know God brought us together, ordained it, established us in heaven, and sealed us with His Holy Spirit. We are totally committed and absolutely in love.

I set the letter down, feeling a little overwhelmed by what Karla had written. I wondered, *Is this going to work, Lord?* I felt concerned because commitment of this type might be too difficult for Dana—or any other person. I knew the reality of their situation. I sighed and prayed, *Thank you, Jesus, for the relationship she has with You. No matter what happens she's secure. It's Your banner of love that's over her.*

Karla's letter continued:

> Jesus often speaks things into my heart as I kneel by my bed, and I can feel His arms wrapped around me. There are no walls that can separate us from Jesus. Dana and I share that same kind of intimacy. And you know what? I am really thankful that we are building our relationship and love on spiritual things first! Maybe if I was out there and we got married right away, physical things would get in the way and slow the process down. But as it is, we are firmly grounded, rooted, and cemented in the spiritual foundation of Christ.
>
> All that we share is built on *Him* and centered around *Him.* Kind of like going to marriage counseling for a few years *before* you put the marriage on paper! But it is our Lord who is counseling us. He did such a warp-speed binding, bonding, and meshing of our hearts. I really wish I could explain it to you better. It is so hard for people to comprehend. Shut your physical eyes and look through your spiritual eyes and feel what Jesus has done. It is totally supernatural and *awesome!!!* We are *complete in Him!!!!*
>
> And like you said, Dallas, when we focus on Jesus and realize He is the only One who can fulfill us completely, then He will work in our marriages and help us with our mates, flaws and all.
>
> We will let each other down at times and hurt

each other. Jesus is the only One who never lets us down. When we don't expect our mates to be perfect and are willing to work through our flaws and accept one another, it becomes the perfect relationship. Then we become knit together, strong and tight. Well, you know way more about marriage counseling than I do, but this is so wonderfully awesome and fabulous!

Had I handpicked someone, or made out the "perfect" list of who I wanted, I would not in a million years have selected a man so perfect for me. But since I wasn't looking, and God handpicked him, he is exceedingly, abundantly, above and beyond all that I could have ever imagined!!!

God knew better than I did who was perfect for His daughter Karla! And He also knew who was perfect for His son Dana! He certainly hadn't gone to prison, much less Life Row, looking for a helpmate!

I put Karla's letter down again and pondered this news. I had to laugh. When people come to us for marriage counseling, Dallas often says, "Infatuation is a temporary state of insanity." All marriages take work and Karla and Dana were already aware of that. But I would see Karla grow into more maturity as she and Dana faced pressure from others who were unable to understand their love. Her letter went on:

> Oh, I did want to share one more thing. We are going through Henry Blackaby's workbook, *Experiencing God*, in our weekly Bible study. We've learned that there will be times when we will have to make

> major adjustments in our lives if we are to join God in
> what He is doing. I learned this with Dana. Some of
> our closest friends did not support our decision to
> marry. Some even parted from us. That is very painful
> for me.

Although many friends questioned their decision to get
married, Karla and Dana were convinced that God had
given them His blessing.

◆ ◆ ◆

As Karla and Dana's wedding day approached, there was
a heightened air of excitement and expectancy on Death
Row. Karla's intense scrutiny of Scripture to determine
God's perspective on marriage influenced each aspect of
the ceremony. Because Karla was on Death Row, she
and Dana could not be physically present in the same
room for their wedding. Karla would have a proxy stand
in for her at the official, legal ceremony. A proxy would
stand in for Dana at the ceremony in the prison. Nevertheless, Karla wanted her wedding day to reflect, as
much as possible, a typical wedding. She used her lim-
ited resources to create a festive celebration right on
Death Row.

Karla made handmade invitations for each woman on
the Row. On a top sheet, she drew two intertwining
lovebirds—one blue, one pink. Underneath the birds
she printed "The Gift of Love." A small, folded piece of
toilet tissue separated the two sheets, which were taped
together. On the bottom sheet, she wrote:

This is to joyfully invite _____
to attend the wedding of
Dana Lane Brown and Karla Faye Tucker
on June 24, 1995, at 11:00 A.M.
Dana and Karla will bind on earth
what the Lord their God has already bound in heaven—
their holy matrimony—
becoming one in the Lord Jesus.
Please dress formal and may the Lord bless you as you witness
His awesome miracle of love!

Before the ceremony began, Karla had told Pam (who would be standing in for Dana), "I was completely fulfilled in Christ before I met Dana. So he didn't fill any void in me. He is an extra blessing from Jesus and I am so glad He is allowing me to experience this love and oneness with another human being. I never, even in my wildest dreams, imagined there could be a love so pure, wonderful, and awesome. With Jesus, yes. But I never knew it was possible with another person. Amazing!"

Turning to Frances, who was standing in as the minister, she had said, "I want to be with Dana all my waking hours—hear his voice, touch him, and share everything with him and have him share himself with me. He is my best friend as well as my husband-to-be. He is my confidant and everything God ordained him to be as my mate." It had taken courage for Karla to embrace Dana with her whole heart. But Jesus had empowered her to risk loving. She must have been a radiant bride.

Meanwhile, Dana was at a hotel in Waco with his wedding party. Included were Art and Aileen Jones, dear friends of Dana and Karla, and Cheryl Archer, the women's staff chaplain Karla had met at the Harris County Jail.

"Karla and Dana had coordinated everything," Pam told me, "with each portion of the ceremony precisely timed. At the precise moment the wedding ceremony started in the hotel in Waco, we began here. It was quite moving. Karla cried and I cried too, seeing her cry. After the wedding she waited at the door, watching excitedly through the small window for Dana to drive up. We waited until after their visit to begin our reception."

At the hotel, Aileen Jones was Karla's proxy. When I met Aileen months later, she told me, "I remember visiting with the girls on Death Row when Karla intertwined her arm in mine and said, 'Aileen, will you do something for me?' She asked if I'd stand in for her at the wedding and I told her, 'Karla, you know I'd do anything I could for you!' And since I had recently been married myself, I added, 'I'll wear my wedding dress, too!'"

Then Aileen told me she suggested that Karla write something personal to Dana so it could be read at the wedding, just as if she were there. Karla agreed.

"A funny moment happened just as we stood up to begin," Aileen said. "My husband said, 'Hey, Dana, in most weddings there's someone who gives the bride away.'

"'Art, that's a great idea.'

"'Well, just remember, buddy, I'm giving your bride away, not mine!'

"We laughed. We had such a good time. We all wanted it to feel like a wedding reception with cake, punch, and nuts! We even threw the bouquet—and Cheryl caught it! Dana was going to leave right after the reception for his visit with Karla, and one of his friends was going to drop him off. I told him that I'd ride with my husband. Everyone laughed when Dana looked shocked and said, 'You get in here with me! You think I'm going to ride from Waco to Gatesville in a car with two men in the back seat with a "Just Married" sign on the outside?'

"We pulled into the main parking lot at Mountain View and we could see Karla heading toward the visiting area. She was handcuffed, surrounded by male guards, but she looked radiant! I couldn't wait for her to see me in the wedding dress. I hurried out of the car and headed toward the fence, laughing, prancing, curtseying, and Karla was joyous. She was smiling, laughing, giggling. The guard in the tower was tolerant for about five minutes. Then he yelled through his bullhorn, 'Get back to your vehicles immediately.'

"Dana waited as they unlocked the gate, then went in to spend time with his bride and we left."

✦ ✦ ✦

In a 700 *Club* interview in 1996, reporter Kathy Chiero stated, "Both Karla and Dana expressed a hope, an impossible hope outside of a legal miracle, for a future together outside prison. Dana explained the basis for his confidence, 'I know that the Lord spoke to my heart. He told me, *If you'll walk through the circumstances, I'll deliver Karla into your arms.*'"

For years after Karla and Dana married, they experienced resistance and separation from people they had been close to. Our acceptance was important to her. In one of her letters she wrote:

> From my heart I say thank you to the whole team for touching my life the way you have, for embracing me as one of the family (for embracing all of us as part of your family), and for making such a big difference in my life. Also, it would not be complete if I did not thank you for embracing my husband, for accepting with open and loving hearts and spirits that it was God who put us together.

Karla kept telling me how much she wanted us to have a relationship with Dana. We were family, as he was, and she wanted us together. In a letter, and during our 1996 visit, she asked us to contact him. During our first telephone call we talked for over an hour. In subsequent conversations he kept us updated on the status of her case. We met with him when we traveled to Gatesville for our annual seminar in 1997.

Karla's heart to see marriage reflect Christ's love came through in a letter she sent to a number of friends:

> Dana and I encourage you to cultivate a burning desire in your heart to search out and create new ways to continually express your love to your spouse, family, friends, and most importantly, your Creator and Savior. Let them know how special they are to you.
>
> With a smile, a hug, or a kind word of praise, encourage them. Let them know how grateful you are

that God has chosen them to be married to you, or to be in their family, or have them as their friend.

Express your love and thankfulness to God, and then see how He causes your heart and spirit to mount up and soar! Don't hold back a compliment or a sincere word of praise. In sincerity and honesty, build up your spouse, family, and friends. You may not have another chance if you don't do it today. . . .

Above all, be joyful in glory, sing aloud to God on your bed, in the shower, in the car, in the bathroom, at school, at work, and everywhere. In the morning, noon, and at night let the high praises of God be in your mouth and a two-edged sword (the Word of God) be in your hand!

Praise God! Praise God! Praise God!

Karla lived what she believed. She believed with all of her heart that the plan of God was for the body of Christ to be one. She allowed God to use her transformed life as a bridge between the body of Christ in prison and the body of Christ on the outside.

In the Old Testament book of Joshua, Rahab the prostitute is portrayed as a woman transformed by her faith. Demonstrating her trust in God, she placed a scarlet cord in her window, and as a result, her entire family received God's deliverance and salvation. Later, she became the mother of Boaz, who married the Moabitess Ruth, and is listed in the lineage of Jesus Christ in the

New Testament. Generation after generation was affected as a result of her act of faith.

In the same way, Karla—a prostitute and murderer at the time of her arrest—came to trust Jesus Christ for her salvation. Like Rahab, Karla became known as a woman of great faith. Countless numbers of people—both those behind the fences and those on the outside—came to understand the grace of God in an entirely new way as a result of her intimacy with God.

The next three chapters recount the stories of a few of the lives touched by inmate 777.

The author (left) and Diana Keough.

Chapter Five

A Bruised Reed
He Will Not Break

But we have this treasure in jars of clay to show that this all-surpassing power is from God and not from us. . . . We always carry around in our body the death of Jesus, so that the life of Jesus may also be revealed in our body.

—*2 Corinthians 4:7,10*

Truly forgiving someone who has hurt you, and finally releasing them, is like God coming down, reaching deep into the depths of your heart, ripping out all the bitterness, anger, and resentment, and just throwing it away.

—*Karla Faye Tucker*

I n 1990, the Texas Prison Fellowship director resigned and Chaplain Crosby asked us to bring in a ministry team under the auspices of our ministry Discipleship Unlimited. We quickly realized that our team included Karla. In one of Karla's letters, she wrote:

> If you only knew how much of a blessing you are to us! The excitement and anticipation that falls over this unit when we know you are coming is incredible. I

know that while you are here God is going to break the yoke of bondage in *many, many* lives.

What touches the depths of my heart is how you have become *family!* You come in here and you embrace us, not just as part of the body of Christ, but also as family, as one of the team. You have a way of letting us know that our prayers for you are just as important as your prayers for us. You embrace us as one of you! And that makes more of a difference than you'll ever know.

In the weeks just before a Gatesville seminar, our Bible study would step up its prayers for the needs of the women-in-white and the team traveling to Texas. On Death Row, the women would begin praying specifically for what God wanted to accomplish, not only in their lives but in our lives as well.

Over the years I've learned that whenever I don't know what else to do with someone—I've prayed every prayer, said all that I know to say, read everything from the Scriptures that is appropriate, and they still haven't found peace or healing—I ask them to come to prison with us. And so it was with Chris. She was a dear friend who was involved in my women's Bible study in Milwaukee for several years. This is the story of how God used Karla and the other women on Death Row to influence Chris's heart and family.

✦ ✦ ✦

Always impeccably dressed, with beautiful jewelry for

every occasion, Chris had been married to a prominent attorney, and the two of them were well known in the Milwaukee area. They had been charter members of many conservative churches, the last being a large church on Milwaukee's far west side. Chris was outspoken, bright, and well-read. She prided herself in being ferociously independent. She was also dying of AIDS.

She had contracted the AIDS virus from her husband, who had led a secret life as a homosexual for more than twenty of the thirty-seven years they had been together. He was now in a hospice in Ohio. She harbored so much rage and anger toward him, it spilled over and contaminated the rest of her life. Sometimes when we were praying, her rage would flare up, and we'd have to stop. She couldn't go any further.

Because Chris had gotten to know my mother over the years, I would often use my own personal battle with forgiveness as a teaching illustration. I told her of my mother's response when I shared that my dad had finally turned to God the year before he died. I had been elated. My mom, on the other hand, said that if my dad were going to be in heaven, *she* certainly didn't want to go there.

I also told Chris about a weekend I spent alone with the Lord. I had asked the Holy Spirit to bring back the memories I was clinging to that were allowing unforgiveness to fester. As I began to forgive my mom, I asked God to apply the balm of Gilead—a biblical term for "healing salve for the soul"—onto each memory that was holding me back. I then asked God's forgiveness for the judgments, words, and punishment I'd inflicted on others because of those who had hurt me. It was then that I realized my biggest issue was self-righteousness. I felt like an impostor—acting loving while my heart was cold.

I prayed, *Forgive me, Lord, even as I forgive those who have hurt me. May my heart and actions be one. Heal me, O God. You promised "a bruised reed you will not break."*

I told Chris that soon after I had prayed that prayer, I was confronted with a choice: Was I going to walk in that forgiveness or was I going to go back and wallow in unforgiveness? I took a step of faith. I invited my mom over for dinner, but then out of the blue, she began criticizing my father (who had been dead for several years). Instead of defending him like I usually did, I left the room. To my amazement, she followed me and asked if something was wrong. I quickly prayed, *Help me, God. What do I say to her?* My response amazed me.

"When you criticize my dad, I feel like you are rejecting me as a person," I said. It was then that I realized I had been protecting myself as much as I had been defending my father. With unforgiveness out of the way, I was able to articulate the truth.

"Something happened in my heart on that weekend of silence with God," I told Chris. "He entered into the pain of my relationship with my mother. I began to see her as a person, rather than just my mother, and then I saw her struggles. He set me free from my patterns of resentment, bitterness, and self-righteousness. Before that weekend, I hadn't noticed those patterns. I was stuck. With God's grace, I was willing to once again risk loving my mom, to begin again to build a new relationship. We had been in the chains of unforgiveness and they were being shattered."

Chris seemed to want that same freedom. After hearing my story she said, "I don't think I can get there. It's out of reach for me."

That's when I had decided to ask her to come to prison. Because she spoke Spanish, I asked her to help us minister to the Spanish-speaking inmates. She said yes right away.

In Gatesville, Chris was assigned a room with volunteer Carol Harris, who lived in Milwaukee's central city and came from a different ethnic and cultural background. Despite the sharp contrast, Carol would have a profound impact on her life.

During that particular weekend, our emphasis was on forgiveness. After interpreting one of the small group sessions into Spanish, Chris walked up to me, crying. "God set me up for this, Linda. These women have been so abused, and they're the ones telling me about their guilt." Then she added, laughing through her tears, "And, of course, I have a couple of girls struggling with homosexuality. Can you believe this?"

✦ ✦ ✦

After the final morning session, I had the volunteers bring their small group to the front. As Chris interpreted into English her group's thanks to her and their appreciation of the freedom they'd received, she had to allow long pauses to maintain her own composure. Before leaving the unit that Sunday, Chaplain Crosby arranged for Chris, Carol, and me to go to Death Row.

I was aware of Chris's outspoken political views on

capital punishment and knew it was a risk taking her there. But we were walking onto what Karla called holy ground. As I often did, I asked Carol to sing. With a passion coming from deep within, Carol began. The familiar words "We are standing on holy ground" filled the small room. Karla, Pam, and Frances gracefully signed the song, with deep reverence, affirming their belief in His presence. Chris was visibly moved.

After listening to the inmates share for about thirty minutes, Chris asked the women, "What could have kept you women from committing these heinous crimes?"

There was a long moment of silence, then Pam answered. "I've asked myself that question many times." She proceeded to tell us about what she called her "normal" childhood—how her father had sexually abused her after her mother abandoned them. How her mother died in a car accident the year after she disappeared. How after being placed in eight different foster homes Pam was sent to Juvenile Hall at the age of ten. Chris was flabbergasted. Later she said to me, "Pam called her childhood normal?"

As we prepared to leave Death Row, Karla knelt down beside Chris and prayed for her. She didn't ask Chris any questions; she just wanted to extend love to a hurting new friend. The walls of Chris's heart fell.

"If God could love these women and forgive them their horrible and unspeakable crimes, then He must also love my husband and extend His forgiveness to him too," Chris realized. And this time that truth seemed enough.

Soon after that, Chris's husband died in a hospice in Ohio.

✦ ✦ ✦

Four years later, in 1994, I answered my phone on a hot June day. It was Diana Keough, Chris's daughter. Diana lived in Ohio, where I knew Chris had been visiting the past few weeks. Now she was telling me that Chris was ill. Diana had put her mom on a plane that morning in Cleveland not knowing if she'd have enough strength to get off once it landed in Milwaukee. She said that she'd been calling her mom's house all afternoon and couldn't reach her. She was beginning to worry.

"She knows she doesn't have much time left," Diana sobbed. "I never should've let her get on that plane, but you know how she can be. I just have to make some arrangements here and I'll be in Milwaukee as soon as I can. Can you get people to help her before I get there?" I assured her I could. Before we hung up, we prayed together.

The day after Diana's frantic phone call, I drove to Chris's condominium. My friend was clearly ill.

"I'm dying, Linda," Chris said. But there was something she desperately wanted to know before she died. "How can I know for sure I've forgiven my husband?" she asked me. Without waiting for me to answer, she continued, "When I was visiting Diana, I read all of his journals. He had written so much about how much he loved me and how sorry he was for what he did." I could see the grief in her face. "He was tormented because I couldn't forgive him and knew he was probably going to die without receiving my forgiveness."

I wouldn't offer her pat answers, only earnest prayer and God's Word. Before we had communion together, I placed a crucifix in her hand as a visual reminder of what Christ went through for the sins of the world. It seemed so fitting. He alone could identify with her suffering. *A man of sorrows, and acquainted with grief. We all, like sheep, have gone astray. Each of us has turned to his own way.* She took the crucifix in her hand and placed it over her heart.

Together we gratefully drank from the cup of suffering representing the blood of Jesus. Then we ate the bread of Life. She thanked Jesus for His body, broken for her. She pointed to a small object on her dresser. "Please, Linda. Take this to remember this day," she told me. I picked up her gift—a rock decorated with a lovely hand-painted cross that she had bought on the streets of her native Mexico. It fit neatly into the palm of my hand. That was the last night she would spend in her own home. The next morning she was admitted to the hospital.

After a week in the hospital, she was diagnosed with cancer and sent to a hospice. By that time Diana had arrived. I had often prayed with Chris for her family, but I was unprepared for how quickly I felt one with them. When people suffer together, barriers come down. There's no pretense. Our time together reminded me of the intimacy I experience with the women on Death Row.

The three weeks spent with Chris and her children,

awaiting her death, remain a treasured memory. Chris would ask to hear the tape of Carol singing "Holy Ground," and other great hymns, over and over again every day. And Diana asked her to retell her encounter with Karla. One night, as all of us held hands and prayed around her bed, she opened her eyes and remarked, "This is so wonderful. Am I awake or am I dreaming this?"

Once Chris and Diana had been estranged, but now their relationship began to heal. Diana stayed with her mom from early morning till late at night, bringing her water, fixing her pillow, attending to her every need. One night after leaving the hospice, we talked for over an hour in the parking lot. She told me, "For the first time in my life I know my mom likes me."

✦ ✦ ✦

My phone rang in the early morning hours of August 1, 1994. It was Diana calling to tell me her mother had passed away just a few minutes before. There was a soft rain coming down and I decided to go for a walk. As I walked the abandoned streets of my neighborhood, I raised my hands and shouted, "Hallelujah! Chris is home with you, Lord. The battle is over." Then I dropped my hands and whispered, "I'm going to miss you, my friend. You fought such a good fight."

Chris and I had planned her funeral, but it went way beyond my expectations. The church was packed with family, friends, doctors, prominent attorneys and businessmen, members of the racquet club, and curious neighbors. I had committed to sharing the gospel with those in attendance.

At the beginning of the service, I held a reed in my hand and read one of Chris's favorite verses: "A bruised reed he will not break. A smoldering wick he will not snuff out" (Isaiah 42:3).

"Chris was not broken," I said. "Instead, she was made into a lovely flute, used to play praises for an Almighty God."

As I continued with the eulogy, I told of our trip to Gatesville and Chris's encounter with Karla. "Chris went on Death Row and met the women there. Those women are alive today and Chris has gone home. We're all on Death Row. We will all die. And it's important to Chris that you, her friends, know where you are going."

I told them that by visiting Death Row, Chris learned that everyone is a sinner and needs a Savior. We all come with a sack of sin. Some have a bigger sack than others. But all sin requires a payment. Jesus paid for sin with His blood on the cross. Then I invited them to pray a prayer asking Jesus to come into their hearts and be their personal Savior.

Chris's six children participated in the funeral and shared highlights of the three weeks in the hospice. Diana told how she had read her mom's Bible every day during that time. A few hours before her mother's death, she discovered a handwritten statement inside the front cover of that Bible. "Mom met Karla when she was facing an execution date. She was surprised because Karla did not seem moved by it. As she discussed her future,

Karla told her, 'Don't be sad, I know where I'm going.' That's what I found written in her Bible."

Before Diana returned to Cleveland, I asked her if she would be interested in going to meet Karla in February 1995. I knew it would help heal the deep wounds that were in her heart. She had experienced so much loss at such a young age. She smiled, asked if I was serious, and then said yes.

Six months later, I accompanied Diana through the many security doors leading to Death Row. She was quiet as the doors slammed shut behind us and I could feel her trembling. But before the fear of the unknown could overtake her, I saw Karla running across the day room, with her arms wide open. The women had been praying for Diana and were overjoyed to meet her. "After all your mom's told me about you, I feel like I know you," Karla told her, as she led her over to the bench.

The impact of hearing that her mother would have talked about her deeply touched Diana. She couldn't stop staring at Karla as she talked. "So this is what you and my mom meant by saying that this place is holy ground," Diana said. "I get it. I finally get it."

She asked Carol, "Would you sing 'Holy Ground'? Mom loved that tape. It seemed to help her so much during her last days in the hospice."

As Carol sang, Diana began to cry. The inmates surrounded her, knelt at her feet, touched her, and began praying. I leaned over and whispered, "Diana, a bruised reed He will not break."

Top: Dallas (left) and Terry Strom.
Bottom: Terry Strom (left) and close family friend Terry Meeuwsen.

Chapter Six

Beauty for Ashes

I will repay you for the years the locusts have eaten. . . . You will have plenty to eat, until you are full, and you will praise the name of the LORD your God, who has worked wonders for you.

—Joel 2:25,26

That same weekend in 1995 when Karla and Diana met, Karla helped bring healing to another person very close to my heart: my son, Terry. Terry had come a long way to be visiting Death Row that year.

Terry was my son from my first marriage, and his early years were marred by pain and trauma. However, after we were established in a loving church in Minneapolis, he seemed well-adjusted and was a delightful child. In 1971, after being Christians for seven years, Dallas and I joined the staff of Campus Crusade for Christ (CCC). In 1973, we were transferred. We loaded our three sons, Terry, Tom, and Steve, and all our possessions into a U-Haul truck and moved from Minneapolis to Whitefish Bay, a suburb of Milwaukee. Dallas was the CCC city director, and soon we were extremely busy with our new ministry. The boys were equally busy—active in hockey, school activities, and with friends.

Terry turned thirteen that summer and we began to experience conflict. Sometimes, when tensions were high and schedules were hectic, we wrote notes and left them around the house. One of mine said, "Dear Terry: This is the first time I've ever been the mother of a teen-ager. I know I've made some mistakes, but I want you to know I love you. I'm always here for you."

One night Terry and I were talking about his most recent struggle. Then the conversation shifted to his spiritual life. Finally, in frustration, he said, "Mom, I know in my head what you've told me about the Lord, but I don't feel it anymore in my heart." He seemed distant and withdrawn.

In December 1975, in the middle of Terry's sophomore year, we felt him slipping away from us. He was at a crisis point. We turned to my brother, Larry, for help. If anyone could give Terry guidance, it was Larry. His search for a relationship with God had begun during our turbulent growing-up years. At Westminster College in New Wilmington, Pennsylvania, he had come into a deep, personal relationship with Jesus Christ. He had served at a mission hospital in Sierra Leone, Africa, and was now a doctor at Kentucky State Prison in Eddyville. He was my hero and greatly affected my life as I watched him live his faith. I knew he could help my son, and he agreed to try.

Terry couldn't believe we were sending him to Kentucky for a semester; it reopened childhood wounds and left him vulnerable. But after he arrived in January, it wasn't long before he met Al, an older inmate who lived outside the prison walls. His position was similar to a trustee, but he slept and worked in the sewage plant. During the afternoons, he was permitted to fish from the bank of the Kentucky River. An avid fisherman, he taught Terry how to catch the white bass and sheepshead that swam in the reeds near shore. Al became Terry's first real friend in Kentucky.

At his new school, Terry lied about why he was living in Eddyville. "I got busted for using marijuana," he told his new classmates. That lie was going to lead him to his first major crossroads. News traveled fast, and he soon found himself with Rick, a student who ended up giving Terry his first joint.

The first marijuana cigarette was no big deal to him. But when he smoked the second one, he got high. The reaction was totally different than anything he'd heard about in youth group, school, or at home. Unexpectedly, it wasn't a bad experience; in fact, he liked it.

After that, Terry experimented with whatever drugs came his way. The Bible says there is pleasure in sin for a season, but he was unprepared for the price he would pay. It would take many wasted years before he would be drug-free.

❖ ❖ ❖

The next fall Terry was a junior at Whitefish Bay High School and he became known as a Door Three Kid. Door Three was the side door where kids who smoked marijuana and didn't fit the preppy profile congregated. I knew he was in trouble and I tried to fix things in any way I could. I fasted. I took him to evangelistic meetings. I arranged for him to meet evangelist Nicky Cruz. Sometimes we skipped school together. I was looking for a miracle—or a quick fix. None was to be found. Finally I persuaded him to see a Christian counselor, Tom Peterson.

Tom met with Terry seven times. Then he called me. I was shocked to hear him say, "Your son knows exactly what he's doing. And he's okay with it. Now I'd like to see you."

The next week I drove to his office. After giving a brief outline of my history, I went right to the point: "I feel like such a failure as a mother."

Tom was quiet for a moment, then he looked over his glasses at me and said, "So you're telling me your son is a failure."

"No, I didn't say that."

But as I contemplated what he said, I wondered, *Am I conveying that sense of failure to my son?*

"I have so much fear," I said. "I always feared alcoholism would kill my dad, and it did. Now I fear drugs are going to do the same to Terry. I've tried everything."

"What have you tried?"

I had gone over my list so many times, it came instantaneously.

Tom listened attentively. Then he said, "You've tried a lot of things. Let's sit for a moment and think if there's anything else."

It was quiet for much longer than I could stand.

Finally I broke the silence. I looked at him and said, "Well, did you think of anything?"

"No, did you?"

I shook my head no.

"There is one thing you can do. You can surrender."

Didn't he realize how vulnerable my son was? And what a dangerous place he was in? Didn't he know I had to fight for him? *And I'm paying him for this!* I thought as I walked to my car. I pulled over on the side of the road and put my head down on the steering wheel. *God, is that what you want? Do you want me to let go of my son? He's only seventeen.*

I wrestled with that question for several days and finally realized I had no choice. That's what God was telling me to do. But would I do it?

During the next weeks, I'd look directly in Terry's eyes every night when he came home from school to see if he'd been smoking. If they were clear, I was happy. If I knew he was high, I'd be hurt or angry. The little girl who once looked out the window to see if her dad was sober was now policing her son. He was in control of my life. Finally, in desperation, I decided, *I'd rather have the Holy Spirit be in control and be joyful—or, if not joyful, at least self-controlled.*

One afternoon when he came home, I decided I'd never check his eyes again. The chief executive of the FBI—the Family Bureau of Investigation—had retired. But I realized that surrendering him wasn't going to work unless I told him what I'd decided, and why.

After greeting me and grabbing a snack, he sat down on the couch in the living room. I joined him and began telling a story about a mother who'd cut off her apron strings and mailed them to her son who was in college. "No one wants to be controlled by another person. Even though I'm struggling with this, I want you to know I've surrendered you to God. I'm releasing you. I can't control you, and I don't want to try anymore. I love you, but I'm letting you go."

Those questioning dark brown eyes looked at me. "You can't do that!"

"Oh, yes I can. I have to surrender."

Still, guilt continued to call me. I'd replay old memories of his early childhood and his time in Kentucky over and over in my mind. Just as I had blamed my mom for my dad's alcoholism, I blamed myself for my son's drug usage. In those moments I turned to Luke 15, the story of the prodigal son. The tears that fell there wrinkled the pages of my Bible. I claimed the promise of a son reunited with his family. When our prodigal son returned, would we have a party!

One night a few weeks later, I was still struggling to receive God's offer of grace. Then a memory of an experience with our middle son, Tom, came to mind. He was three at the time and had thrown a rock through a window in our storm door. Devastated, he told me how sorry he was. After cleaning up the broken glass and wiping his tears, I sent him back outside to play.

Over and over that day he would run back inside to apologize. He'd say, "I'm sorry, Mommy. I'm so sorry."

Eventually, I stooped down beside him, put my hands on his shoulders, looked him square in the eye, and said, "Tom, don't you understand? I've forgiven you. It's over."

I so much wanted him to accept my forgiveness and not bear the heavy load of guilt he was carrying. God brought that memory back to me and said, "That's you, Linda."

That night, Terry was late getting home and my imagination ran wild. The truth of what God was teaching finally gripped me. I immediately got out of bed and got on my knees. *God, a long time ago, You forgave me. Yes, there are consequences, but You've taken away all my sin and guilt. Now, just like I put my hands on Tom's shoulders, affirming my love as he struggled with his feelings of guilt, please place Your hands on me.*

I knelt there until I heard the front door open. I went down and told Terry, "Something wonderful has just happened to me."

"What happened, Mom?" he asked. No matter where he was in his rebellion, he was usually so kind and concerned about the effect he was having on us.

Tears were in my eyes as I answered. "Tonight I finally received the forgiveness that God offered me a long time ago—and that you've been offering me. I know I'm forgiven." The tears in my eyes were now tears of joy.

He looked at me for a long time, his eyes searching my face. "Oh, Mom, I'm so glad. I feel so guilty about what I'm doing, but I feel most guilty about what I'm doing to our family."

Chains between us were being broken. We hadn't known how to do it ourselves, but God was doing it for us. He was honoring His promise in Matthew 16:19: "Whatever you bind on earth will be bound in heaven, and whatever you loose on earth will be loosed in heaven."

The summer after his graduation, we encouraged Terry to visit his natural father in Pennsylvania. He had not seen him in ten years, and we felt this visit might bring healing. Yet the thought was always in my mind: *Will he come back?* I also couldn't help but see this as a test. Had I really surrendered him?

Terry was nervous, knowing it would be another turning point in his life. Before he arrived, he imagined seeing a stranger. However, when he walked in, he stopped. His father was sitting at the table. *He looks so much like me,* Terry thought as his dad walked over to give him a welcoming hug.

By the end of the visit he realized his dad loved him. But he also knew he didn't fit there. Deep down, he knew he was a Strom. At the age of twenty, while he was living a lifestyle totally opposite ours, he approached Dallas. "Dad, you wanted to adopt me when I was three and you've been a wonderful father to me. Now I'd like to ask you, Can I legally change my last name to Strom?"

Dallas felt honored by his request. When Terry was three years old Dallas had gone through the adoption process but the adoption was denied. At that point, Terry had been an adorable little boy—straight black hair and big brown eyes. Now at twenty he was a drug user and had walked away from our values. Yet the father loved the son and wanted to claim him as his own. This moment reminded us of the adoption we have into the family of God. He chose us before the foundation of the world, but there comes a day when we need to choose Him, just like Terry chose Dallas. Now the adoption was complete.

It wasn't yet time for us to throw the party; Terry still was having his own pleasure in the far country. There, he met his wife, Jean. Before their wedding she indicated she wanted Jesus Christ to be part of her life. Yet during the early years of their marriage we saw little sign of Christian growth in their lives. In 1992, our first grandson was born. We were at the hospital when Terry said, "Dad, we've named our son Jacob Dallas after you."

He seemed tired of wandering in the far country and vacillated between walking the walk of faith and yielding to defeat. In spite of his struggles, he talked to many of his friends about Jesus. Then he would direct them to us. He had seen God work in our lives, so when he got stuck in a situation he'd ask us for help.

One night he called to tell me that his friend Jim, a heavy IV drug user, had committed suicide. That suicide was a wake-up call for Terry. He came to us.

"Jim's dead and no one's sure why, and I'm sitting here wondering what happened. What could I have done differently?" He stopped for a moment. "I feel so powerless."

After talking for over an hour and getting nowhere, I asked Terry, "How would you like to come to Gatesville with us in February?"

He laughed. "Mom, whenever you don't know what to do with someone, you take them to prison. I guess it's my turn. Sign me up."

◆ ◆ ◆

When he came to Gatesville in February 1995, Terry was resigned to his addiction and felt he would never be free. Sitting on the plane with our ministry team he wondered why he was going. He knew he had Bible verses in his head, so he thought, *I can get by, I can do this. But I don't have anything to offer the inmates. The only difference between us is that they are broken and in prison while I am supposedly free.*

Carrying his guitar, he headed to the fenced-in area around Death Row. He saw Karla waving enthusiastically, jumping up and down. She ran to him and gave him the Karla hug.

"Terry," she said, "it's so good to finally meet you. How's Jean? How's Jake? I've been praying for you."

Soon after they started talking, she asked him if he was going to sing. He opened his case, pulled out his guitar, and said, "This song is my story."

> I was born a Christian
> That's what people say.
> My dad was the pastor
> And I was a PK [pastor's kid].
> Friends would laugh at me
> Some would put me down.
> My head started spinning
> Around and around.
> So I'll tell you what I did
> Well, I smoked some pot
> And took some pills.
> I thought I really got
> Some pretty good thrills.
> But no thrill is

Like the one I have found.
Because when Jesus came in
He turned my whole life around.

As Terry sang that last verse, he had no idea how turned around his life was going to become. Karla talked about her struggle with heroin, which began when she was ten. She identified with his battle. Then their conversation shifted. He felt as if he was alone with her.

"I know Jesus fixes broken people," he said, "but I'm not sure he can fix me. In spite of my inconsistent lifestyle, my friends still come to me for help. I tell them about Grampa Strom's influence in my life. I try to explain the power I felt when he would lay hands on me and pray. And of course my mom is my prime example of someone who came out of the pit and got her life together. I know what God did in her marriage!

"Some of my friends became Christians, but then I don't see them anymore. They changed. But here I am, talking about the Lord and the power He has to change lives and my own life is out of control."

"Terry, you sound just like what Paul describes in Romans 7," Karla said. "Let me read the end of that chapter to you." She opened her Bible, which was lying beside her on the wooden bench: "'When I want to do good, evil is right there with me. For in my inner being I delight in God's law; but I see another law at work in the members of my body, waging war against the law of my mind and making me a prisoner of the law of sin at work within my members'" (verses 21-23).

"If God could set me free, Terry, He can set anyone free." Then she quoted Jesus' words: "If the Son sets you free, you will be free indeed" (John 8:36).

Terry left Mountain View on cloud nine and returned to the motel where he was rooming with Big D. He walked into their room saying, "Dad, I'll never be the same after tonight."

They talked most of the night. When Dallas was just about ready to fall asleep, Terry thanked him again for sticking with him through all the years in the far country.

The party had started!

A year later, Terry and his wife, Jean, were greeted on Death Row with Karla's hug and her special Texas "Howdy!" After talking about the change that took place in his life, he sang the song he wrote immediately after leaving Death Row the year before, "I See Jesus in You."

> I walked into that place
> And I could see Him in her face
> His love came shining through
> There was nothing you could do
> But be in awe of You, Lord.
> I see Jesus in you.
> I want to be that way, too.
> All of His glory
> Tells me the story
> That He lives in you.
> There is nothing for us to fear

And I know that He is right here
And when I'm through livin'
I know I've been forgiven
And He'll take me home with Him.

Karla loved the song; it's message was her hope. She knew that what Terry saw in her wasn't about her. Lives were changed on Death Row, but it was Jesus who changed them.

Death Row inmate Pam Perillo; Pam was Karla's cellmate
and friend for the entire time Karla was in prison.

Chapter Seven

Weeping Endures
for a Night

The LORD is close to the brokenhearted and saves those who are crushed in spirit.

—Psalm 34:18

God inhabits the praises of His people. If we are praising the Lord, then the devil has no place. God brings us comfort and healing. We have to realize that we are going to have tribulation. He never promised us it was going to be easy. If you look through the Word you will see that everyone who knew Him went through major tribulations. He said, "My grace is sufficient." We know that He is with us through this and we are able to comfort one another. Praise is a choice. We open our mouths and release praise to Him so He can come in and do in our lives what He needs to do.

—Karla Faye Tucker

The next two years were to be a mixture of intense joy and heavy sorrow as God strengthened our hope of heaven even as He reminded us of the reality of death.

My personal time of preparation for Karla's execution

began with a conversation with Pam. In that same 1995 life-changing seminar during which Diana and Terry met Karla, I spent time with the women on Death Row. They knew Chris, Diana's mother, had died of AIDS in August, and they grieved her senseless death. I emphasized what an impact their lives, particularly Karla's, had on Chris's family. It was as if God pulled back a curtain, giving us a clear view of what it means to be connected in the body of Christ. He had linked our lives together with unbreakable chains of life-changing grace.

After we talked more about the link between us, we broke into pairs for prayer. Pam took that opportunity to say, "Linda, I have something important to ask you."

We sat down beside each other. She pushed back wisps of red hair from her face and said, "You need to think about what I'm going to ask, and pray about it."

Ignoring the activity around us, Pam grew still. "I just had a hearing, and the next stop for my case is the Fifth Circuit. If I lose in the Fifth, there's only one more court to go into—the Supreme Court. They don't accept a lot of death cases anymore, so my chances of being heard there are pretty slim. I'm waiting on this decision, and it's very possible that I will get an execution date."

Pam looked down at the floor. "I'd like you to come to Huntsville with me for my execution." She paused. "You must know I will understand if your answer is no; I know how difficult this would be for you. You don't need to answer me now."

I already knew my response. God had been preparing me for this question. One day in 1992, before leaving Gatesville to return to Milwaukee, I had tearfully waved good-bye to the women on Death Row. Every year it became harder to leave them. They had become my friends, and I knew I wouldn't see them for another year. As I turned to wave one last time, the thought hit me, *Next year when I come back, one of them could be gone.* Chaplain Crosby was beside me. I knew he loved the women, so I asked him, "If one of them goes to Huntsville, you'll go with them, right?" I couldn't bear the thought of any of the women going through an execution without someone who loved and cared for them being there.

I was surprised when he said, "No, the system has specific, strict guidelines for each step of the execution process. I can't be with them. But there is a good chaplain at the Walls Unit. When the time comes, I will be with the family at the Hospitality House in Huntsville."

Something began stirring deep inside me as he continued to explain the process. After that conversation I began asking, *God, is this something You are preparing me for?* Soon I knew the answer: When one of the women faced execution, I would be with her if she requested it. Now it seemed the event God had been preparing me for had come. Pam's blue eyes focused intently on mine. I took her hand and quietly said, "When that time comes, I would be honored to be with you."

❖ ❖ ❖

This wasn't the first time Pam faced the emotional roller-coaster ride Death Row inmates experience upon receiving a date. She had been two days away from her execution several years earlier before receiving a stay.

"That was my hardest time in here," she said later. "I thought I was prepared for my execution, that I could handle it when it came. But once I received the news, I kept thinking about how to prepare my son."

Her son, Joseph, was sixteen years old at the time. When she was arrested, he had been one year old. The last time she held him, he was six. Her new attorney and his wife had taken the unusual step of adopting Pam a year after she was sentenced. They also adopted her son.

"After I received that execution date, the emotions I went through during my visits with Joseph and my mom ranged from laughing together to sitting in shock." With tears in her eyes, she smiled, remembering one visit. "We had such a good time together. I just enjoyed being with my son."

In contrast, another visit was extremely emotional. "As my adopted mom, Joseph, and I were talking together, Warden Baggett walked over to discuss what to do with my body after the execution. It was a very sad visit.

"Besides the impact on my son, I struggled with other feelings when I was alone in my cell. I thought that Christians weren't supposed to fear death since we know where we're going. I didn't fear dying, I feared people watching me die. Satan attacked me in so many ways! I kept saying, 'I can't possibly feel all this fear and still be a Christian.'

"In my most desperate hour, God led me to Jesus' words in the garden of Gethsemane the night before His crucifixion. 'My Father, if it is possible, may this cup be taken from me (Matthew 26:39).' I read that Jesus, too, felt lonely, troubled, and overwhelmed with sorrow. He even fell on His face to the ground, sweating great drops of blood. That truth set me free. God showed me that whatever I was feeling was okay, because Jesus came in human form and experienced the same feelings, fears, and temptations.

"On Friday, two days before my scheduled execution, my attorneys were going to a meeting with a federal judge at 9:00 A.M. I was supposed to be transported from Mountain View to the Ellis Unit in Huntsville that night, since my execution was scheduled for 12:01 A.M. on Sunday.

"Chaplain Crosby was not working that morning, but he called from home and requested permission to speak with me on the phone. He asked if there had been any word from my attorneys. I said, 'No, but we're fixing to come together and pray.'

"He said, 'Well, let me hang up and I'll pray with you from here.'

"We were praying when two officers came to escort me to the visiting room, I was to meet my mom and Joseph, who had stayed to be with me for our last visit. Just as I was walking out the door, the phone rang. It was my attorney. He told me I had been given a stay of execution.

"Instead of saying good-bye that day, I walked into the visiting room and told my mom and son the unbelievable news. We were so excited! We jumped up and down and whooped and hollered!"

Pam later reflected on that tumultuous day and on her upcoming execution date in a letter:

Dear Linda,

I love you so much and I want you to know how much this means to me. I've been wanting to ask you to be with me for a long time, but I just didn't know how. It's not easy to ask someone you love to watch you die! When I had my last death date and I came two days away from it, I felt so alone. I knew I needed someone to look at. I knew in my heart you would say, "I love you Pam. You will make it all the way home." You always make me feel like I can do anything and I'll need that to make it through.

✦ ✦ ✦

As I left Death Row the afternoon Pam and I talked about her execution, I kept thinking about what Pam had experienced before and would possibly face again. Her request was so personal and intimate, I needed to absorb what had happened during our visit and pray.

After spending time alone in prayer, I knew what I needed to do next. I wanted to talk to Mary Stocking, a gentle woman from Milwaukee with an infectious laugh. A contagious spirit of adventure and comfort springs from her creative heart. That Friday afternoon, when she arrived at the motel with the rest of the team from Wisconsin, I was waiting in the lobby.

"Mary, we need to talk," I said as I grabbed her suitcase. I told her about Pam's request and she listened. She knew very well that my grief from Chris's death was fresh. She also understood that Pam's situation was at a critical point, and therefore, my attendance at her execution was a real possibility.

Once we got to her room she prayed with me, as she had the previous summer when my involvement with Chris was intense. She reminded me, "You know how God prepares you, Linda. Now take it one day at a time."

As we finished praying, I wasn't surprised when she said, "If Pam goes to Huntsville, I'll walk with you, Linda."

Before I left Mary's room, I told her she was scheduled to teach on Death Row Saturday afternoon. I knew she bathed each session in prayer long before it started and had a way of making everyone feel safe.

❖ ❖ ❖

Saturday afternoon, Mary met the women in the day room on Death Row. Mary often uses clay to demonstrate God's hands-on involvement when He created us. She began distributing lumps of clay and directed the women: "Shape the clay with your eyes closed, creating your body as it might have been in your mother's womb. Don't judge your work while you're forming it." She added, "This isn't a visual exercise, it's a work of the heart."

She then played an instrumental praise tape while reading from Psalm 139: "For you created my inmost being; you knit me together in my mother's womb. I praise you because I am fearfully and wonderfully made; your works are wonderful, I know that full well (verses 13-14)." Once finished, the women opened their eyes.

Karla gasped with delight at how much detail she saw in her clay figure. "Mary, it's so incredible to think how intricately God is involved in each of our lives. The detail is unbelievable. With what Pam's facing right now, it's a reminder of His mighty yet intimate work in our lives." I looked at the women holding their little clay figures and thought again about the type of death each one faced.

After guiding them through this creative process, Mary compared their work to the way God shapes and reshapes us. "He knows just the right place to apply pressure while conforming our lives to His purposes. Now, bring your clay figures to the table and we'll work together to shape them into one large cross."

Being part of the body of Christ took on a deeper reality as their hands joined to form the cross. Once finished, they used the leftover clay to create Christ's body. While they worked, Mary played another song and the words, "Down at Your feet, O Lord, is the most high place," brought a holy hush.

Karla later wrote, "I trembled with awe and sorrow as I formed His feet; sobbing as healing poured in. I don't know of a better way to complete deep, inner healing than at Christ's nail-torn feet. It is there that the power of His shed blood and His victory over sin is remembered."

❖ ❖ ❖

As I boarded my plane back to Milwaukee the following Monday, I was ecstatic about how God had moved. First I saw a new excitement in my son. Then I knew Diana,

Chris's daughter, was never going to be the same. Next was Pam's breakthrough. After years of holding back, she was beginning to trust. And finally there was Karla's joy. She had an anointing as a shepherd of the little flock on Death Row. She was grateful that Pam had taken the risk to ask me to be there at her probable execution.

Several other events over the next months reminded me, my family, and the women on Death Row, that even in the midst of death and suffering, the promise of heaven is real.

◆ ◆ ◆

A few weeks after that trip to Gatesville, my twenty-eight-year-old nephew Brian died in a skiing accident. Brian was my brother Larry's only son. Waves of grief and frustration, an angry sea of unanswered questions, overwhelmed my family. I was amazed, even uncomfortable, at the depth of my own anger. I felt out of control, like a child having a temper tantrum.

The next month, April 1995, I remained discouraged and grieving when my friend Terry Meeuwsen and I traveled for our third ministry trip to Israel. Terry and I have an honest, safe friendship; it was such a comfort to me to be with her during this time. We arrived in Jerusalem, which was as breathtaking as ever. Yet even as I looked out over the city, heavy grief enveloped me. I thought of Brian and Pam and Karla and the heaviness of death. I could identify with the story of Lazarus and his distraught friends who were weeping for their dead loved one. Then I thought, *Jesus also cried*. That thought was a comfort.

As I visited the places Jesus walked while on earth, He placed His wounded hand on my broken heart and I began to heal. I went to Caiaphas's house and walked down to the bleak, dark, underground holding area where it is believed Jesus was placed while waiting for His trial. I stood there, noticing how small the room was, how lonely it felt—so damp and cold. Talking to Jesus, I asked, *Were you afraid, Lord? It feels so lonely here.* I bowed my head and gradually my tears changed from tears of grief to tears of relief. *You do know the depths of sorrow.*

Terry came and we joined hands and prayed for Pam as she faced her possible execution date, and for Karla and Frances as they supported her. They, too, were in a holding cell, just as Jesus had been.

I remembered a teaching on tear bottles I'd heard at the Biblical Gardens. I've always loved Psalm 56:8: "You have seen me tossing and turning through the night. You have collected all my tears and preserved them in your bottle! You have recorded every one in your book"(TLB). In Jesus' day people kept small bottles, which could be placed under their eyelids to collect their tears. In the Gospels we read about the woman who washed Jesus' feet with her tears. I imagined her emptying the bottle over the precious feet of Jesus, her spilled tears representing the losses in her life.

Releasing our tears at the feet of Jesus is both physically and spiritually healing. It is almost as if grieving tears have an unusual chemical makeup that releases a poison from our system. After Brian's death, my cheeks were so raw from my tears I used salve to heal them. I prayed for healing tears to come to Pam and Karla and myself as we grieved.

After his son died, Larry wrote a poem that expresses what so many of us were feeling:

Faith Is

To believe when there is no answer
To see purpose in the tragic
To keep the vision even in darkness
To envision the possibility of God
To endure as pain demands
To accept unwanted loss
To affirm life fully
To flee not death
To see treasures in each moment of being
To shut all doors to despair
To unite the broken pieces of life
To dare to live again.

◆ ◆ ◆

As my time in Israel ended, I prayed, "I'm not exactly sure where to start, Jesus, or how to do this, but I want to let all this sorrow go." Shortly after I returned from Israel, God began to answer my prayer when my grandson, Jacob, who was almost three, and I decided to go to Kopp's, our favorite frozen custard place. Snow was melting in the warm sun, and the parking lot was packed with Wisconsinites longing for a taste of summer. As Jake got out of the car, he headed for the nearest water puddle. How he loved splashing in them! Amazed at how quickly the muddy water splattered his blue jeans, I took his little hand and we headed inside. The only available seat left was a window ledge. I realized why Kopp's was so crowded when someone walked in with a big, beautiful Happy Birthday balloon bouquet.

Jake took one look at those balloons and decided he wanted to play pretend. Some days he was Captain John Smith and I was Pocahontas. Other times he was David and I was Goliath. But this day he wanted to be Donut Man and I was to be Dunkin. (Donut Man was his favorite video.) He had my attention now.

"Guess what, Dunkin?" he said with great enthusiasm.

"What, Donut Man?" I asked, knowing the script well.

"Dunkin," he said with his beautiful brown eyes gazing expectantly up at me, "Jesus loves water puddles and balloons."

Jacob had sensed my distance and my pain. He, who had taught me so much about play, was inviting me to celebrate life again.

✦ ✦ ✦

Our hope grew over the next months as we continued to look toward heaven. In 1996, several weeks after we had returned from another Gatesville seminar, Karla sent a letter:

> Before I tell you how totally blessed we were when you guys were here, I must share an exciting praise report! God is *so good and so wonderful!!!* Are you ready to shout the roof off???!!! Weeellll, Pam's appeal was

granted in Federal Court! *Hallelujah!* I know she already shared this with you, but *wait!* There is more! We just got *another* praise report a few days ago! I don't know how Pam explained it to you, but basically the federal judge saw all kinds of legitimate errors and granted Pam an evidentiary hearing. Her attorneys told her it could take up to about a year and a half because the State had a right to appeal the decision. But guess what? *Your prayers have availed much!* The State had decided not to appeal, but they, too, want the hearing. *Hallelujah! Thank You, Jesus!* This means she should be going back to the County soon. *Pleeease* keep her *covered* in prayer. This is a crucial time.

As I finished reading Karla's letter I thought again about an *Experiencing God* principle: When God wants us to take a new step or direction in His plan, it will be in sequence with what He has already been doing in our lives.

I realized it *had* been a year of preparing for a new direction. Between 1995 and 1996, my relationship with Karla took on deeper meaning as we began to face death head-on. Karla had stood by Pam as she awaited her probable execution date; she also comforted me after my nephew's death. God was preparing us to face Karla's own death.

In one of my letters to Karla I compared our relationship to that of a birthing coach and a woman in labor:

A woman suffers during labor, but she endures because of the hope of seeing her child. We are also suffering with this execution process. However, our role is reminding each other of the hope of seeing Christ face to face. You're doing a great job of that, Karla. I just came across a writing by Mario Bergner. I know you'll love it. He described how he helped his mom face her death by painting a biblical picture of heaven. I couldn't wait to mail it.

With my letter I enclosed "Hope of Heaven" by Mario Bergner:

Hope of heaven is key in redemptive suffering. My mother died four years ago of cancer. It was very quick acting cancer, but it was also very painful the last two weeks of her life. At one point I asked my mother, "Mom, do you have any images of heaven?"

She said, "No."

My mom was a Christian, but she had never heard a sermon on heaven. Many of you have never heard a sermon on heaven and images of glory are missing from your soul. Without those images there's no pull outside yourself when you're suffering because a lot of the courage to suffer is related to hope, and hope is related to the future, and the future for us is related to heaven.

There's an incredible denial of death in Christianity. Rarely do we hear sermons on death and heaven. So I looked up all the biblical references and pieced together a prayer. I told my mother what I could tell, at least from the Scriptures, about what happens when you die.

Then we would practice dying together. I would say to my mother, "Be careful, don't die on me right now, let's practice together. What I want you to do is pretend that you're like Jesus and you, like He on the cross, have power to do this—you have the power to hang on for another breath of life or to give your spirit to the Father."

This is what I used to pray for her to pretend that she was at the last moment of her life. I told her, "Hold your fists really tight and then open your hands when you think Jesus is coming and say, 'I give You my spirit.' That's all you need to do.'"

' Then I prayed this: "Ma, this will be the last time you can take another breath. Maybe you've got energy for one more, but don't do it. Just go ahead and go with the Lord Jesus. Just decide to give the Lord your spirit and open up your hands. The minute you do you'll feel the separation of your soul and spirit from your body. The angel of the Lord Jesus himself will come and harvest your soul.

"You'll be traveling very quickly until you see the City of Heaven in the distance. It's surrounded by four walls with three gates in each wall, each one carved out of a large pearl. The walls are made of jasper, which is a see-through stone. From within the City of Heaven is a great light and you can see the green ring around heaven, which is the wall of heaven.

"As you approach the City of God you'll come to one of the gates which you're supposed to enter and there is the Book of Life. A page will turn and there's your name written there.

"See, your name written there: Jinette Madeleine Roux Bergner, written in the blood of the Lamb, for that is the ink they use in the Book of Life.

"Someone will call out your name and the gate of heaven will open and you will find yourself within the walls of the City of God. Just as you hear the gate close, if you look down you'll see that you're standing on a golden road where the gold is so pure and refined that it looks like glass. You can see right through it. Then, if you look up into the sky in heaven you'll notice there is no sun in the sky because the presence of God is the light of heaven. Keep walking on the golden road and you'll see that it leads to the River of Life. The water is crystal clear. And on each side are the trees of life and the leaves are for the healing of the nations.

"Pick one of those leaves, Mom, and press it to your heart. Now, let all that pain that's in your heart left over from the war, from the agony of being an immigrant, from the abuse, from the hurt, from your disappointment—all that your heart has suffered—let all of the pain go into that leaf and throw it into the River.

Follow the River upstream and when you get to the source you'll notice that it's coming from the throne, which is the throne of the King of Heaven. There are layers of fine jewels—sapphires and rubies and diamonds—and sitting on the layers of fine jewels with seven lamps and an emerald rainbow about it is Jesus. When He sees you He'll come down off His throne and He'll embrace you. There may be one tear left in your eye, and if you want to Ma, go right ahead and cry that last tear out. He'll wipe it away from your eye.

"Then He'll sit down with you and you'll have dinner together. And in heaven one day there is like a thousand years down here. So, Ma, if you wait for about fifteen minutes we'll all join you there."

As God had taught us over those difficult months and years, "weeping may remain for a night, but rejoicing comes in the morning" (Psalm 30:5). God would continue to prepare Karla and those around her for her upcoming execution. During the last weeks of Karla's life, when the reality of separation became heavy, one of us would smile at the other and whisper, "Remember, it'll be okay. We'll see each other in about fifteen minutes."

Part III

The Journey Home

Sister Helen Prejean, author of *Dead Man Walking* (left), visiting Karla in prison.

Chapter Eight

Treasures in Darkness

I will give you the treasures of darkness, riches stored in secret places, so that you may know that I am the LORD, the God of Israel, who summons you by name.

—Isaiah 45:3

I was in the wilderness, but it was by no means dry, because there's always a well of living water bubbling up. Circumstances don't dictate my joy. The joy bubbles over, no matter what.

—Karla Faye Tucker, 1997

Karla's faith deepened from the time of her conversion to the final months before her death. In late 1996, *700 Club* reporter Kathy Chiero interviewed Karla. She observed, "The Karla Tucker I saw was visibly different than the one I interviewed in 1993. She had a maturity, a depth, a soberness that comes only one way—in a life walked with Christ."

Karla's growth as a Christian began immediately after her salvation. According to Rusty Hardin, a former Harris County prosecutor, "By the time I met her, you had a person who was extremely remorseful. The proof of her change came as I was preparing the murder case against Danny Garret [in 1984]. She did what no other Death Row inmate had ever done. She testified against her co-defendant."

In spite of dropping out of school after seventh grade, by 1986 Karla had earned her high school diploma while in prison. She had also already earned the respect of prison guards who credited her with helping prevent the suicide of two other inmates. During an interview on *Justice Files*, Karla tearfully explained why: "I love life now. Instead of taking lives I just want to share the life in me."

Just as it is for everyone else, Karla's spiritual transformation was a process. "In those first years at Gatesville, I had a deep craving for more of God and for more of His Word. I wanted to be able to walk in victory amid such an adverse atmosphere. But when I had questions, I did not always have someone to answer them. I didn't know how to pray at first and ask the Holy Spirit to illuminate God's truths to me. I kept reading the Bible, but would get frustrated at times because I just couldn't understand some of what I was reading. Yet my joy level was beyond registering on any scale. That kept me going, just knowing the depth of forgiveness and love God had given me. My church family began to teach me the truths of God's Word concerning the body, my righteousness in Him, and the faith, works, and grace doctrines. I had a book list about a mile long to read, which was required for every family member of our church."

Karla feasted on the Word of God. She also devoured books like *Mere Christianity* by C. S. Lewis. Her spiritual growth could be seen as she used the everyday trials of prison life as steppingstones to maturity. Her concern was for others. Being center stage was never her goal.

When one of the new women on Death Row gave her life to the Lord, Karla wrote about what she learned as a result of discipling this new Christian.

> She is fun to share with because as I share things she always asks, "Where is that in the Bible?" So it makes me dig and always be sure I can back up what I say with God's Word. And this is the way it should be: God's Word and what He says should always be our final say in a matter. As a matter of fact, I was just sharing with someone the other day about how we tend to try and make God's Word line up with our own emotions and feelings and opinions about matters and situations, but it should be totally the other way around. We should make our feelings and emotions and opinions line up with God's Word.

> He has definitely taken us into a new season with all kinds of things that will help us grow, if we embrace *Him* and look to what He is trying to do in all of this. Please keep us in prayer as we grow together, learn from each other, love each other, and experience God and His love. It's not always easy. Matter of fact, it gets rather *hard* sometimes.

✦ ✦ ✦

Karla's continued spiritual growth was evident in our 1997 seminar in Gatesville. We were unaware at the time that this was to be our last seminar with Karla.

I had a sense of the importance of the upcoming weekend as I prepared for it. The Lord began speaking specific words into my heart. Some were spoken in quiet whispers, others were distinct and clear. Over and over I heard the words found in John 2:10, "But you have saved the best till [last]." I didn't know what was to happen—what God meant when He spoke those words—but if it was important enough for Him to persist, I wanted to obey. I've learned to respond to God's gentle tap on my shoulder.

I realized part of my response to God's Word was to share what we would experience that year with others. I called John Jones (J. J.), who directs the audio-video ministry at Elmbrook Church in the suburban Milwaukee area, to see if he could join us and capture the work on videotape.

God knows the future and prepares us for whatever it holds. Had I known that this would be our last seminar on Death Row with Karla, I would have been far too emotional. His timing is always perfect. This step of obedience would have life-changing results beyond my wildest imagination.

✦ ✦ ✦

I began to realize the impact this video would have when I sat with J. J. weeks later in a dark production room, condensing the days of videotape into a short, intimate video. After spending much of his free time working on the tape, he said, "Linda, this will be life-changing. Not just for us, but for many people."

The faces of the women I'd grown to love filled the twenty-five monitors on the wall. The video started with Stephanie, an inmate serving twenty years, singing "The Day He Wore My Crown." Then Pam, who is usually guarded and reluctant to show emotion, freely expressed gratitude as she talked about an assignment her son had been given in his Christian school. "Joseph was told to write a paper describing an experience in his life that had given him strength, and he chose to write about me." She and Frances again signed "Holy Ground."

Karla, as usual, exhorted the body of Christ. "My first eight years as a Christian were filled with joy; it was a feast at the banqueting table. Then I needed a physical healing. I knew God was well able to heal me. He can do anything He chooses with a blink of His eye. But He's not always going to do what we want because it's not always good for us.

"I was really sick and He took me out of my comfort zone and said, 'There are people out there going through the same type of thing you are. There's no way you can minister to them if you allow circumstances to dictate your joy.'

"There's a time, I'm ashamed to admit, that I would have said to someone going through this type of thing, 'Get over it. You know the Lord. Get over it.' But through my circumstances He showed me it's not that easy. It was a hard time for me, and the Lord finally had to say, 'What's wrong, Karla? I'm right here with you. Are people seeing you gripe and complain or are they seeing you praise Me? Can you show them that My grace is sufficient, right now, right here?'

"I remember praying in my cell and jumping right up on His lap in the throne room, demanding what I felt entitled to. I'd hold my Bible and declare, 'I'm in a covenant relationship with you. I'm your child. Your Word promises me these things. You're supposed to heal me.' I was telling God how to be God.

"When I finally shut up and listened to Him, He said, 'I will do what I know is best for you. I am God. Let Me be God in your life.' I didn't receive the physical healing I sought, but I did receive an inner healing. It came when I truly surrendered at the foot of the cross."

J. J. and I sat quietly, watching one last time as Karla's image flashed across the screens. I was struck by her range of emotions as she dramatically signed Ray Boltz's song "Thank You for Giving to the Lord." The music and signing ended, but J. J. had continued filming as Karla, still signing, walked over to me. She pantomimed taking her heart in her hands, then she gently placed her hands over my heart and hugged me. After we embraced, she signed "I love you" and hugged me again.

"J. J." I said, "you have captured the heart of what's going on in Gatesville."

We had no way of knowing that in less than a year clips from that video would appear on such national television networks as Fox, CBN, MSNBC, and on public and even foreign stations. Karla's joy and contagious faith, captured on tape on Death Row, captivated audiences from *Good Morning America* to *Larry King Live* and in churches and prisons across the country. God has used that video to take the message of hope in the face of death to the world.

❖ ❖ ❖

While the video continues to have a wide impact, it could not capture all of the events and emotions of that weekend trip to Gatesville. We did not know it at the time, but that seminar would be Karla's last visit with volunteer Mary Stocking.

One Friday evening service, Mary told us we would be focusing on the Father-heart of God. "Our picture of God as Father has often been distorted by our fathers' actions," she said. "We need to know what God is like."

We began the evening by discussing the story of the prodigal son in Luke 15. In this story, Jesus revealed God as a waiting, watching, and loving Father. We were reminded that God is eager to receive us. When no one else celebrates us, He throws a party. He takes us as we are—we don't have to clean ourselves up first. As God's children, we can joyfully proclaim, "Abba, Daddy, I belong to You." Our heavenly Father's love is genuine, warm, and dependable. It is a solid love that heals us.

Mary handed each person a lump of moldable clay. She said, "Jesus wants us to know and experience the Father's love. Think about the crucifixion and all that He did to open the door for us to receive His love. Now, take your clay and create something that reflects what your heart is saying in response."

Once we finished, she asked each one to explain what they created. Frances formed a crown of thorns. "He is my King of glory," she explained.

Karla shaped three crosses. She held up the first cross. "Jesus is on this one," she said. The second cross also had a clay figure on it. "The thief is on this one." Then she held up the third cross and explained why it was bare. "I'm the murderer that should be on this cross, but instead it's empty. Because Jesus died, I'm here today—alive and free on Life Row. He wasn't forced to the cross. He chose to die for me, a murderer."

Dallas reflected on the reality of death as he sat with the women sent there to await their execution. He struggled silently with the awareness that this was preparation for a future day. There was no glib talk about the crucifixion. If Jesus hadn't made it to the cross, suffered and died, there would be no hope, no Life Row, no courage to face the painful reality of a pending execution.

Dallas himself had made a crown without thorns. "I see Christ on the other side of the crucifixion," he said. "When we are with Him in paradise, we can worship Him and cast our crowns at His feet."

With a twinkle in her eye, Karla laughingly expressed what Dallas couldn't. "We women share in the pain of the crucifixion, but Dallas skipped right over it and went straight to the victory!"

As we left the prison, I had an underlying sense that things were changing.

◆ ◆ ◆

In July 1997 Karla wrote:

> About a month ago my appeals were denied in the Fifth Circuit Court. We are now getting ready to appeal to the Supreme Court. We don't anticipate any

relief there. Therefore we are also in the process of preparing to petition the Parole Board and Governor for a commutation. To be granted, this would truly be a miracle from God! And then all would have to confess His Name and confess that *His* mercy pardoned me! I am not real sure how the process in the courts works, as I have always left it in God's very capable hands to guide my attorney and give him wisdom. So this is all I know to share with you.

Man's report says it looks grim, but God's report says we are just beginning. Dana and I have been given a promise and we stand firmly on it without wavering! We say, with Shadrach, Meshach, and Abednego, our God whom we serve is well able to deliver me from the fiery furnace and He *will* deliver me! But if not, let it be known that we will continue to serve our God and sing His high praises and share the hope we have and the reason for it. We never give up or bow our knee to defeat or hopelessness. We know that death has lost its sting on us (and *all* who have given their lives to Christ). We are only on a pilgrimage on this earth anyway, until the Lord has completed His plan in our lives and calls us home! Hallelujah!

Dana and I appreciate your continued prayers.

While her letter caused concern, and calls went out to our prayer chain, I wasn't afraid because we'd gone through this process before, most recently when Pam's appeal was granted.

Four months later I stood in my bedroom, numb, the phone at my side, asking myself, "Can this possibly be happening?" We had just moved into a new home and were anticipating the Thanksgiving holidays with our family when the phone rang on November 1. "Linda, this is Warden Baggett. Karla's received her execution date. She wanted to know if you and Dallas could come here to be with her. She understands that you might not be able to because of the financial commitment."

She paused, then added, "But Karla and I will feel most comfortable if those who are with her now are already in a long-term relationship." Karla later told me she had prayed, "God, they are way up there in Wisconsin, but I want them here. Please send them to me, God."

I was speechless. I'd been up and down this road before. Yet I still felt unprepared for Karla to receive another execution date. My thoughts raced, and a long, emotional, roller-coaster ride began. Would God take her home or would He leave her with us? Should we expect the obvious and go with our feelings of grief—and then rejoice if He left her here? In both instances she would have God's victory. If she were executed, she would be with Him. If she were granted a stay, she would continue ministering to prisoners, volunteers, and even officers—within Gatesville's walls.

While my heart recoiled at the thought of her being executed, I also thought, *Surely they won't execute a woman. They couldn't possibly do that.* After all, it had been over 100 years since a woman had been executed in the state of Texas.

I didn't want Warden Baggett to hang up, but what could I say? What should I ask? After eleven years of being involved on Death Row I felt like there was much more I needed to know. What was going on down there? How were the other women dealing with the news? After a few long moments, I regained my composure. "How is Karla dealing with this?"

I could hear her struggle to maintain emotional control as well, as she walked the tightrope between her professional role and personal concern. "You know Karla," she replied. "She asked me, 'How can I make this easier on you, Warden Baggett?'"

During the weeks following Warden Baggett's phone call, she made arrangements for me to move freely about the institution. She issued an interoffice communication to her staff, giving me permission to go on Death Row and anywhere else within the prison, the typical access of a volunteer chaplain.

❖ ❖ ❖

After Karla received her execution date, she requested a transfer from Death Row to the Isolation Unit. Some might not understand such a choice The Isolation Unit was just what the name implies. Inmates spend twenty-three hours a day in cells so narrow they can reach out and touch opposite walls. Heavy steel doors seal the cement block rooms. Guards slide food through a lower, locked slot underneath a narrow window of about twelve inches. Inmates leave their cells an hour a day for exercise and to shower.

Karla moved out of the dorm on November 16 at 9:00 P.M., two days before her thirty-seventh birthday.

Because of the unique situation, the women were allowed to remain together and celebrate her birthday with a party.

And a party it was. There was much laughter and joy. They had learned to celebrate life. Karla's last day on Death Row was no exception. Her friends knew she wanted them to remain joyful. It wasn't until she opened her gifts (purchased out of their meager funds) that they broke down and cried.

Karla knew her decision to leave was right. She could not remain focused on God's purposes if she stayed there and watched her friends suffer.

In November, Aileen Jones, who had stood in for Karla at Karla and Dana's wedding, sent Karla a letter:

> When Dana called us about your possible date, he said, "Don't give up, Aileen." I assured him and now I am assuring you that I will never give up because I believe in the omnipotence and sovereignty of our God. I wouldn't blame God one bit if He wants you with Him (you are so very precious to Him), but we surely do want Him to let us have you with us for the same reason. He will reveal His plan, and it will be the very best. We trust Him with you.
>
> Your precious Dana keeps us informed about what is going on—*60 Minutes,* etc. He shared today that Governor Bush's representative said at a meeting where Sister Prejean [author of the book *Dead Man Walking*] was speaking that the governor is very interested in viewing the *60 Minutes* program regarding you. That is good news!

Dana and I spent hours on the phone during December when I was back and forth between Wisconsin and Texas. I knew my role was far easier than his. He was on the battlefield and left nothing undone. At times he seemed near exhaustion. I could hear the panic and pain in his voice. During one phone call, Dana said, "Linda, I think Karla's tired. She doesn't want to fight. I'm not ready to give up. I feel like Joshua on the battlefield and I want to see victory."

I knew Karla wasn't fighting to save her life. The primary reason she was going through the commutation process was for countless other lives. In her January 1998 letter to the Board of Pardons and Paroles she had stated:

> I see people in here in the prison where I am who are here for horrible crimes, and for lesser crimes, who to this day are still acting out in violence and hurting others with no concern for another life or for their own. I can reach out to these girls and try and help them change before they walk out of this place and hurt someone else. I am seeking you to commute my sentence and allow me to pay society back by helping others. I can't bring back the lives I took. But I can, if I am allowed, help save lives. That is the only real restitution.

It wasn't that Karla was giving up. If she was going to live, she knew there was a purpose, a plan for that. In either case, her focus wasn't her, it was communicating the love and forgiveness that she had experienced.

I reminded Dana that while Joshua and his army were fighting the enemy, Moses stood on the hill overlooking the battle, his arms outstretched in prayer. Dana knew the story well. Every time Moses' arms became weary, Aaron and Hur were there to support him. I assured Dana that people everywhere were lifting up both him and Karla in prayer.

Dana realized Karla was already looking toward heaven. She was leaving him. She told me, "I love Dana so, but I am ready for our time to just stand. I couldn't have fought this good fight of faith without him. He brought something I didn't have to the battle. I hadn't planned on going on national television; yet, because of him, the message of Christ's forgiveness has gotten out. He has been my rock in all of this, just as Jesus is our rock."

In the weeks ahead we all would lean on that Rock of Christ as we faced the reality of Karla's death.

Chapter Nine

The Battle Belongs to the Lord

Some trust in chariots and some in horses, but we trust in the name of the LORD our God.

—Psalm 20:7

God is doing something so big we can't even begin to know what it is. It is for His glory. I remember when Gideon was facing a vast multitude. God said, "Cut your army down to three hundred because when you go out there, I want people to know it's Me who wins the battle." In my life or in my death I want that, too. We don't know what He is going to do. I think one of the reasons He doesn't show us is because He only gives us grace for today. He will give us grace to do what we need to do. He is moving in a lot of lives out there. He knows whether He is going to reach more lives through this happening or through stopping it. That's okay, isn't it? That's what we want.

— Karla Faye Tucker

I n December 1997, Karla had told her friends Mary Alice and Charlie Wise about her desire for me to be

Karla found sign language to be a valuable ministry tool.
Here she is making the sign for "I love you."

with her during her final weeks. Then she had said, "Mary Alice, I have a favor to ask you." Charlie and Mary Alice were family to Karla. For years they had spent every Tuesday evening in a Bible study with the women on Death Row.

"You can ask me anything," Mary Alice replied. In the five years she had known her, Karla had never made a personal request before.

"Dallas and Linda Strom live in Wisconsin and I know it's difficult for them to travel back and forth. Could they stay with you and Charlie during some of the remaining time?" After their conversation, Mary Alice called Milwaukee and invited us to stay with them as long as necessary.

Tim Crosby, who had left his chaplain position at Mountain View some months earlier, was the pastor at Trinity Baptist Church in Gatesville. Knowing I'd be back in town, Tim had asked me to speak at the Sunday evening service on January 11, 1998. Again I saw God's perfect timing: We needed to pray during Karla's final days, and the church members would pray for us that evening.

After church, Tim and his wife joined us for a four-star meal at the Wises' home. As we talked that evening, Mary Alice and I realized we had both been approved to record videos of Karla Thursday morning. Mary Alice quickly deferred to me: "I'm sure your video should take priority," she said. "We'll just have to reschedule ours." Her self-sacrificing attitude stunned me. I would live with the Wises during a highly tense and stressful period of our lives. In all our hours together, I saw the same devoted Christianity I had seen in Karla.

Although we had the video of the 1997 Gatesville seminar, Karla had ideas for two more videos. She had given both of us outlines of what our videos should contain and of what she hoped they would each accomplish. She wanted me to produce a video for "those behind the fences." She wanted another video to send a personal message to the prison volunteers who had meant so much to her over the years. Her request came in a letter written on December 10, 1997:

I write with a special purpose. It is 12:30 A.M. and I have been fellowshipping with the Lord for the last two hours, having a great conversation! He put something on my heart about fifteen minutes ago and I asked, "But how, Lord? How can I get this done?" I realized you guys are coming next week and I just might be able to do this with your help! What I want to ask is if there is any way you can bring a camera in and allow me to share my heart? There are two things in particular I want done.

One: Make a tape to send to Governor Bush. Two: Make a tape to send to Al Gonzales, one of the governor's general counsels. When Mr. Gonzales came here with the chairman of the Parole Board last week, I shared an idea with him for a program that I believe will help people in our prisons. He said to write it up and send it to him. My mind is racing with all the things I am trying to get done, it's so hard to write a letter right now. It would be so much easier if I could share this on tape.

The outline for Mary Alice's video was five pages long and very detailed. Karla had told her, "The body of Christ in here is not complete without the body of Christ out there. God's remnant behind these fences is a part of the whole, and we need our brothers and sisters to help us. People who come to Christ in prison need to be connected to the body when they go home." Together with Tim Crosby, Mary Alice would produce a video featuring Karla's testimony with the hope of encouraging churches to adopt an inmate.

As Mary Alice and I talked, I said, "Karla is walking this out with an assurance that nothing in the world will interfere with what God's called her to do."

"Her sense of adventure is contagious," Mary Alice said. "But the thing that affects me most about Karla is the way she completely disarms people with the love of God. I have never met anyone with such all-out love for Jesus." We sat around the dining room table until nearly midnight sharing stories about Karla and her effect on our lives. Then Charlie suggested we pray for each other and get some rest.

✦ ✦ ✦

I was thankful to be staying in a quiet, peaceful home rather than a hotel. Because of family and ministry obligations, Dallas and our son Terry would not be joining me until the following weekend.

After walking with me to the guest room that was to become my haven, Mary Alice opened the drapes. The Wises' home is located on a hill overlooking a valley. I stood in awe. Lights from the prisons below stretched across the entire horizon, filling the sky, overwhelming the silhouettes of the houses across the street.

Karla's down there, I thought. Somehow, seeing those lights, I felt closer to her. *I can see right where you are tonight, Karla. You are just one small person in that massive system, yet you are so loved by God and by His people.* The prison was so near, yet so far. I prayed silently, *Oh, God, please be her strength and comfort. Help her not to be lonely.* Mary Alice put her arm around my shoulder. We knew we were in this together for the long haul.

By the time I got under the blankets, it was 2:30 A.M., January 12. As I do most nights, I wrote in my journal. "I am very weak, Lord. You are my strength. Would You give me a word for Karla, Father? Our eyes are on You! We want You to be glorified on February 3, yet now I strain to hear Your voice."

As I lay half-asleep on my bed, tired from the day's events, the story of Joshua before the battle of Jericho started playing in my mind. Joshua had been apprehensive. Jericho's walls were so solid, strong, and high. He must have felt overwhelmed. So God sent a messenger dressed in battle gear. He knew Joshua could relate to a soldier. As I thought about this, I prayed, *God, You know us intimately. You know exactly how to meet us right where we are.*

I sat up in my bed, grabbed my Bible from the table, and turned to Joshua, chapter five.

Having someone near you with a drawn sword is a great comfort when you know he's on your side, but Joshua needed to be certain that this was the case. He asked the man, "Are you for us or for our enemies?"

The angel replied, "Neither . . . but as commander of the army of the LORD I have now come."

"That's it!" I said aloud. "The battle is not about us. It's all about Him!" Karla's life wasn't in the hands of the governor or the prison system. Every legal avenue was being pursued to get a reprieve, but the State did not have the final say. The Lord was in control. He has come!

✦ ✦ ✦

The next morning, driving alone to the prison, I thought about the Joshua verses. *Are they just for me, or am I to share them with Karla?* I wondered.

I entered the Isolation Unit and went to the reception area where I sat down behind the crash gate, waiting for the officers to unlock Karla's cell. Finally she walked down the corridor toward me. She usually had a bounce in her step when she walked, but there was none that morning. As soon as I saw her, I could tell that she had something heavy on her heart. Her expression seemed to say, "I am leaving you." With intensity in her voice and her eyes fixed on mine, she asked, "What are you going to tell them, Linda, if God takes me home on February 3?"

I remembered what Warden Baggett told me earlier, "She's like a mother with a list of important things to accomplish and a deadline for them to get done." Karla's question was obviously on that list. I responded by explaining how God had prepared me during the night for this very question. "Let's read Joshua 5:13-15 together," I said.

> Now when Joshua was near Jericho, he looked up and saw a man standing in front of him with a drawn sword in his hand. Joshua went up to him and asked, "Are you for us or for our enemies?"
>
> "Neither," he replied, "but as commander of the army of the LORD I have now come." Then Joshua fell facedown to the ground in reverence, and asked him, "What message does my Lord have for his servant?"
>
> The commander of the LORD's army replied, "Take off your sandals, for the place where you are standing is holy." And Joshua did so.

After reading this passage, we sat in silence for several minutes. "These words affirm what you've been saying, Karla. Your life is not in the hands of anyone but God. He's here—but for more than just being present. He's here to take over." Over and over during the next weeks, in interviews on national television or in conversations, Karla would stress, "My life is not in Governor Bush's or the Parole Board's hands. It is in God's hands. Either God is sovereign or He's not. And He is!" That Monday morning, fingertips linked between the mesh, we grew still as an awareness of the presence of the Lord surrounded us, transforming the Isolation Unit to holy ground. Quietly, without speaking to each other about what we were doing, we slipped off our shoes. Paying no attention to the tears streaming down our faces, we began thanking the Lord for the sense of His presence. In times of stillness, He imparts His strength. This must be what it means to "be still and know that I am God."

After our moment of silence I told her about my time of prayer with Mary Alice the night before. Karla was delighted to be the link between us. She told me, "I knew that one day you would love each other." I think she also knew the great comfort we would be for one another in the days and years ahead.

"Karla, miracles are happening all around us. This morning was unbelievable. Jeanne Rogers from *Life Today* called to confirm that a camera crew will arrive on Thursday."

Karla's eyes lit up. I saw her mentally cross off another item on her to-do list.

I continued, "Jeanne volunteered to come down from Fort Worth on Wednesday with her assistant. Jeanne's a fabulous worship leader and she offered to minister in music. I said they could come but that no programs were planned. You won't believe what happened next, Karla! Just as I hung up the phone, it rang again. This time it was Chaplain Nelson. He told me that we've been granted permission to hold a prayer vigil for you in the chapel Wednesday. Look how God provided our worship leader!"

She smiled. She loved seeing God's fingerprints in everyday details. It seemed to bring her courage for the challenges that lay ahead.

"Every passage of Scripture is coming alive to me," I went on. "This morning I was reading about Queen Esther and I decided I'd talk about her at the vigil."

Turning to the book of Esther, Karla and I marveled at the young queen's courage. What motivated this beautiful woman to go before the king without invitation, knowing that if he did not extend his scepter she would die? Her words, "If I perish, I perish (Esther 4:16)," took on a new dynamic for us. She was not sentenced to die, as Karla was. She had not harmed other human beings; she voluntarily put her life on the line. Why would she do this?

Karla answered our question slowly, thoughtfully. "For the people. . . . Yes, for her people. Take this to the women. The world is watching us. We need to let them know that God is the same in the hard times as in the good times. Pray that we will glorify Him in what we say and do."

She was identifying with Esther. She had willingly submitted to authority and forcefully challenged the other women to do so, too. Her life was in the King's hands. Her people were the men and women behind prison fences.

By her response to pressure, it was obvious Karla had used her time in prison to mature as a Christian. As she grew spiritually, God began to develop her into a Christian leader who led by example. She didn't tell us to be joyful; she was joyful. She didn't avoid the reality of her execution; she faced it with courage, confronting any fear. She didn't try to get people to pray for her life to be spared; instead, she challenged us to glorify the Lord no matter what.

She told me, "I fear God more than I fear what man might do to me. Since I fear God, I don't have to fear anything else. If I do not fear God, I would fear everything else." She had modeled how to live before us and now she would demonstrate how to face her execution with humility, love, and dignity. For several more moments we sat in silence.

I thought about the twenty days left until her execution. For the last month, when I was restless and unable to sleep, I would fight my fear with Bible promises. I knew the Bible didn't say we would never struggle with fear; instead, Psalm 56:3 says, "When I am afraid, I put my trust in Thee" (RSV). During the night hours I wondered if Karla, too, felt afraid. As I thought of her locked alone in a six-by-nine concrete cell, behind a steel door with only a tiny window, she seemed isolated, vulnerable, and helpless. "Karla, are you able to sleep?"

She seemed surprised that I had asked. "Oh, yes! At night, when I'm locked in my room, I worship God. I sing to Him and I pray. It's so wonderful, His presence. I thank Him for loving me and I let Him know how much I love Him, too. As I worship Him, His glory fills the room, and in His presence I fall on my face before Him. Then I sleep.

"It's the prayers of God's people, you know," she explained.

Karla knew others were praying. On national television, 700 *Club* host Pat Robertson had expressed his support for her. Co-host Terry Meeuwsen rallied people from all over the world to pray. Likewise, our Discipleship Unlimited volunteers had formed a prayer chain throughout the country. Churches such as Trinity Baptist were praying at their services. Even the Pope sent a request to the United Nations, requesting their intervention.

Brothers and sisters inside the fences have prayer chains, too. Their network is incredible. Many times I walked into the Gatesville chapel and saw the women gathered in small groups, praying. Other times, while walking to the Isolation Unit, inmates would see me and say, "Tell Karla we're praying."

We knew we were in God's school of prayer, experiencing firsthand the overflow of corporate prayer. Corporate prayer transformed Karla's small, cold isolation cell into a holy room where God's child enjoyed solitude with her Creator. Corporate prayer brought believers together in one accord, casting their differences aside. Corporate prayer broke through the crash gate's steel bars; unable to hug physically, we learned to hug in the Spirit.

I frequently thanked God for the privilege of seeing Him so obviously at work. The effect of this corporate prayer spread throughout the institution. What preparation for a prayer vigil.

✦ ✦ ✦

At 5:45 P.M., Wednesday, January 14, the prayer vigil began. Tammy Williams, the chaplain's inmate secretary, had spread the word and the chapel began filling with women. Karla knew many of them and had discipled some through the fenced-in exercise area outside Death Row.

As other women entered the chapel, some knelt briefly at the altar rail before quietly sitting in the hard oak pews. It was a serious, subdued time. Fran Turner, the prison beautician and one of Karla's close inmate friends, gave me a letter she had written to Dana in December 1997. It was presented to the Texas Board of Pardons and Parole, and was going to be read at the "Save Karla" rally in Austin, Texas, on January 17. Now I read it to the women.

> Karla is the prime example of an entirely changed individual. She is not the same person who was sentenced fourteen years ago. She is responsible for many of our conversions—and the positive changes in our lives.
>
> I have known her all these years. I was blessed to be her steady pen pal, and to speak with her on a regular basis when the wardens approved. . . . We've laughed and cried together, but no matter what, we always ended our visits praying together. She has been my rock! My Paul!
>
> She is the one I clung to when I felt I couldn't make it in here another day. When Mama got cancer and suffered for so long; when she died and I couldn't go to her funeral; it was Karla who explained the system and made me understand why I couldn't go. Then everything seemed all right. . . .
>
> They [the Parole Board] have to know what's been going on in her life over the past fourteen years. She has been in a cage. She's had every right to be depressed, hopeless, even bitter at times. Yet she's

completely forgotten about herself, and instead she's used this time to help us get our lives back together. She wants us to go back out and be good mothers, good wives—decent citizens.

She's encouraged us to go to school, get good grades, so none of us will ever have to come back here. When she saw no hope of ever getting out—no hope for herself—her only concern was that we ladies out here in population get saved, get our acts together, and prepare to go home. No one could fake that attitude.

Dana, don't worry. I won't say anything against the system—far from it. Coming here was the best thing that's ever happened to any of us. Besides, Karla obeys all authority. She's made us promise that no matter what, we'd be orderly and obey authority to the fullest.

After I finished reading her letter, I looked out at the women. We were together in one accord. Spanish-speaking women joined hands and hearts with English-speaking sisters. Black hands and white hands gripped each other for comfort and support. Faces, blotchy from tears, were wiped with sheets of toilet paper passed from woman to woman throughout the chapel.

I was deeply touched by the guards' kindness. A gray-uniformed officer placed a hand on the shoulder of a weeping inmate. Another sat down in a pew beside one of the women and spoke a word of hope. The sweet communion of the Holy Spirit and the fellowship we were sharing momentarily removed us from our surroundings. Jeanne led us in a time of praise and worship. Standing in the chapel that night, we experienced the true meaning of the song "You Are My All in All."

> You are my strength when I am weak
> You are the treasure that I seek
> You are my all in all
> When I fall down You pick me up
> When I am dry You fill my cup
> You are my all in all.

After worship, while everyone was standing, I told a story about my little grandson.

"When Jacob was a toddler, he and his PaPa, Dallas, routinely walked across the street to play on a steep bank. Jake would pick dandelions while his PaPa sat on 'Killer Hill.' After a short while, Jacob inevitably became bored and began a new game, rolling down the hill. He wouldn't realize how far from his PaPa he had rolled. He would stand up on his wobbly legs, look up that giant hill, stretch out his hand, and say, 'PaPa! PaPa!' Immediately Dallas would pick him up, hold him snug and secure in his loving arms, and carry him safely home. Like Jacob, we are children with weak, wobbly legs. We need strong arms around us. Father God is here for you tonight. He's here for me and He's here for Karla. He is our strength when we are weak."

Just before our prayer time I explained that Karla and I had discussed Queen Esther and the courage she demonstrated in the face of death. I told them, "Courage does the right thing in spite of fear. We are suffering, and suffering brings people together in prayer. Prayer brings a yielded heart and words of passion like, 'If I perish, I perish.'"

And out of the pain of that moment, the little chapel became a house of prayer.

◆ ◆ ◆

Several days after the vigil, Karla wrote Fran the following letter:

> I saw the prayer vigil. *Wow,* it was awesome. I sat and cried as I watched and I kept my hand on the screen as the prayer time was going on. It was so neat to be a part of that—from right here. Our warden really has a heart for all of us and wants to see us do good. Keep her in prayer. I believe she was appointed by God to be here at this time (for such a time as this)! Frannie, please make sure to let her know, after February 3rd, how thankful everyone was to have her standing with us.
>
> Honey, please let all the girls know how much I love them and that I am praying for all of them as we go through this together. No matter what happens February 3rd we must give God all the glory and praise!!! It is imperative we do this. Share Acts 20:24 with everyone. ["However, I consider my life worth nothing to me, if only I may finish the race and complete the task the Lord Jesus has given me—the task of testifying to the gospel of God's grace."]
>
> I hope to give you a hug in person soon. If not, I'll hug you in heaven. May the Lord our God send an

extra army of ministering angels with His Holy Spirit to help comfort everyone should I go home. And the same army to help us dance and shout should I stay. Dance and shout for joy even if I do go home.

Karla and Ron Kuntz; Ron uses his photography to minister to prisoners and their families. He took treasured pictures of Karla two months before her execution.

Chapter Ten

Embraced by Love

You're blessed when you feel you've lost what is most dear to you. Only then can you be embraced by the One most dear to you.

—Matthew 5:3, THE MESSAGE

I know that justice and law demand my life for the two innocent lives I brutally murdered that night. If my execution is the only thing, the final act that can fulfill the demand for restitution and justice, then I accept that. . . . I will pay the price for what I did in any way our law demands it.

—Karla Faye Tucker in her letter to Governor Bush and the Texas Board of Pardons and Paroles, January 1998

After I began staying at the Wises' house, I started a daily walking routine. I left the house at about 7:30 A.M. and turned to walk through their beautifully landscaped subdivision. Each morning, at the same place, a dog barked as I passed by. From various vantage points I could see the prison, and I used the solitude to talk with God. Deep grief often surfaced during these early morning walks, and I freely opened my heart to my Father.

With each passing day, Karla's leaving became more

of a reality. Sometimes I felt great frustration about the commutation process and the Texas Board of Pardons and Paroles. I spent long hours working on an affidavit with Karla's attorney, only to find out that several of the eighteen members had voted against commutation before they ever read our petition. Yet because of Karla's intimacy with Christ, and the almost bridal-chamber atmosphere that surrounded her, I could not voice my frustration to her. She wouldn't have listened, anyway. Her focus was on Him. I felt helpless. *Do You know what this feels like, God?*

As though God hadn't heard me, I cried out again, *God, do You know what this feels like? Knowing the exact hour your friend, who has become like a daughter, is going to be executed—the pain is so deep. Do You know how much I hurt?*

The tears accompanying my prayer brought some relief. I emptied my heart to God and continued walking quietly. From deep within, I heard the Lord's still, small voice: *I do know your pain and how deeply I feel your anguish. My Son, the perfect Lamb of God, was executed for you and Karla. I, too, knew the exact hour. Oh, the pain of that moment—turning My face from My Son broke My heart.*

I stopped and looked up toward heaven. I had never viewed the crucifixion from the Father's perspective. Grabbing a tissue from my pocket, I wiped the tears from my face and cried, *Oh, God, I'm sorry. I'm so sorry, Father.* He *did* know. The situation was in His hands and He could be trusted.

I shared my experience with Karla and we sought to

express our gratitude to the Holy One. Christ, who was perfect, suffered while the Father's heart broke. That's when we decided that we must have communion together before Karla left for Huntsville to be executed. The crucifixion and resurrection were taking on new meaning for us. In our emotional poverty, we found ourselves spiritually rich. We were finding in God the peace, comfort, and joy that is deep and strong and real enough to take us all the way to His place. Karla modeled this for me, but now I was owning it myself.

Meanwhile, Pam was working tirelessly to gather support for the "Save Karla" rally in Austin on Saturday, January 17. Since Karla was receiving so much coverage in the media, Pam hoped that a large crowd would sway public opinion as well as the Board of Pardons and Paroles. Her hopes were high that the body of Christ would respond to Karla's plight. After sending out hundreds of flyers to churches throughout Texas, she was expecting a large percentage of Christians to turn out for the event.

The rally, like everything else surrounding my journey with Karla, was filled with conflicting emotions. Jesus said people would know us when they see His love in and through us. His love melts hearts of stone. A picture of that love was seared into my memory at the rally.

Dallas, Terry, Charles, Mary Alice, and I drove to Austin. Instead of a large crowd, we discovered a small, very diverse group of less than five hundred people. The media were well represented, with at least twenty-five national television reporters. However, to our surprise, the Christian turnout was sparse. Bianca Jagger, a member of the Amnesty International leadership council and the former wife of rock legend Mick Jagger, spoke passionately, as did other death penalty opponents. Late in the afternoon, Karla's attorneys addressed the group, surrounded by people carrying signs with Karla's picture.

Then Dana walked toward the microphones. After speaking for just a few moments he had to stop, overcome by emotion. A man who had been standing behind him walked over and placed his hand gently on Dana's shoulder. While we waited for Dana to regain his composure, the woman next to me asked who the other man was.

"That's Ron Carlson," I said. He was the brother of Debbie Thornton, one of Karla's victims. He was also Karla's friend, and he had visited her often over the years. Throughout the last few weeks he had become a familiar face in the media, sharing his story during numerous television interviews and appearing on a *Larry King Live* panel discussion that had followed Larry King's interview with Karla. Ron had worked closely with Dana and Karla's attorneys in their efforts to have her sentence commuted to life in prison. Karla had asked him to be one of the witnesses at her execution.

"I was twenty-seven years old, heavily involved in drugs and alcohol when my sister Debbie was murdered," Ron told the crowd. "When I learned how she was murdered, I was immediately filled with bitter hatred for the people involved.

"I did not attend their trials, but through that entire ordeal I wondered how anyone could do such a horrible thing. My hatred continued growing. I was asked to appear in the courtroom when they sentenced Daniel Ryan Garret to death. I still remember talking to the gentleman handling the case for the State of Texas. 'He got the death penalty. Is that what you want?'

"I replied, 'He got what he deserved.'

"I continued using drugs and alcohol, trying to drown my pain. My sister was dead, yet my conscience kept telling me that my hatred was wrong. I knew two wrongs did not make a right. My hating them put me in the same place they were. If I would have had a chance I would have killed them myself. I read the transcripts and looked at the evidence, including all of the photographs of the crime scene. I saw the dead bodies lying on the mattress, so I am well aware of what happened that night.

"My natural father, William Gerald List, was murdered in August 1984, a year after Debbie. (I was adopted along with my sister when I was five years old.) He was shot with a shotgun at close range. Again, I could not believe what was happening and I kept sinking deeper and deeper into despair and a feeling of life's worthlessness.

"This pattern of behavior went on until about 1990. A good friend of mine, who was also my dealer, gave me a Bible that had belonged to my natural father. I read it for about six months and was doing great until I learned that Christ had been crucified. When I read that, I said to myself, 'I cannot believe it—they even killed God.'

"I closed the Bible and didn't read it again for at least thirty days. The pain still ate away at me, and my hatred continued to build. I picked up the Bible again and started to read the Gospels. I learned that Christ died for our sins and rose from the dead and went to be with the Father.

"One night I was ready to kill myself. Instead, I got down on my knees and prayed, *Lord, I'm at the end of my rope. I can't deal with all of this anymore. Please take over my life, take away the pain, and replace the hatred with Your love and compassion.*

"I also asked God to help me get out of the terrible lifestyle that I was leading. Soon after that, I felt a desire to contact the people who destroyed what little family I had. I didn't know how to do it. I just knew that I had to make peace with them. I was told by people within the prison system that I would have to write to the prisoners and tell them that I wanted to visit them. Because of pride, I would not write them, even though the Holy Spirit commanded me to do it. I continued to resist until an opportunity arose in 1992 to visit Karla Faye Tucker one night at the Harris County Jail.

"She was in Houston for an evidentiary hearing on her case. A man I knew kept telling me about her conversion although he doubted her sincerity. I doubted it too. Nevertheless, I went to the jail and requested to see Karla that night. To my surprise, I was allowed to visit with her for about fifteen minutes. She did not know why I had come to see her.

"She immediately began to sob and hid her face. She was definitely ashamed of what she had done. I interrupted her and told her, 'Karla, whatever comes out of this, I just want you to know that I forgive you and that I don't hold anything against you.' I immediately felt a great and powerful weight or burden had been lifted off of my shoulders."

✦ ✦ ✦

In the difficult weeks following the rally, we needed close friends beside us. When Jesus walked to the garden of Gethsemane, He took Peter, James, and John with Him. They were His "garden friends." Although I could not fully relate to the deep sorrow Jesus felt that night, I could relate to His desire to have close friends near. While in the garden, Jesus made an appeal to His Father for His life as His friends slept nearby, unaware of the depth of His pain. In contrast to what Jesus experienced, Karla and I were aware of the need to pray for each other and were grateful for our safe, loving friendship.

On Monday, January 19, I drove from Gatesville to Dallas to pick Terry Meeuwsen up at the airport. Terry has been my garden friend for over twenty years. Since 1987, each time I returned home from Mountain View, I shared Karla stories with her.

On Tuesday, Karla and Terry spent an hour together in the visiting room. Though separated by Plexiglas, the bond of love that had begun in prayer solidified as they met face to face. Their conversation was videotaped and would later be shared with hundreds of thousands of 700 *Club* viewers.

Terry asked, "Karla, are you afraid of dying?"

She replied, "No, I'm not. I know where I'm going. I know that Jesus has already gone to prepare a place for me, and that He'll come and personally escort me home. Because I believe that, I have no fear. I don't worry about myself. But I am concerned for those who are going to be left behind: my family and friends, my husband."

"We don't know what God's plan and purpose is in all of this," Terry said. "There are a lot of us praying for you, Karla. I think about everything that's been in the media lately. I had to laugh the other day because we've looked at the gender issue, we've looked at politics, we've looked at the death penalty—so many issues. Then I turned on a program and they were talking about advocacy journalism. I just shook my head. I thought, 'We don't get it.' It's not about any of those things. In truth, it's not even about you. It's all about Him."

"You're right," Karla said. "It's not about any of that. It's about God's redemption and the blood of Jesus and the power of God to change a life. It's about what Jesus did on the cross."

"And that'll be true whether you're commuted or whether you're executed."

Karla nodded. "My desire is that God is glorified in either my life or my death."

As their time together was ending, Terry sang "Amazing Grace" while Karla signed. As she signed the last verse—"When we've been there ten thousand years, bright shining as the sun, we've no less days to sing God's praise than when we first begun"—she lifted her eyes toward heaven. She folded her hands and bowed in an eloquent curtsey before the Lord. In the holiness of that moment, one of the watching prison officials from Huntsville said, to no one in particular, "None of this makes sense."

✦ ✦ ✦

Later Terry told me, "Karla is so confident and grateful about her future. She knows heaven is her destiny, and just like everyone else, I am the one who feels encouraged." That evening, even though we were tired, we decided to drive back to the prison. Terry had been cleared to go into Death Row.

As we walked into the day room, Terry saw the cells straight ahead as I had described. Above us, a guard was stationed in the cage. Another guard was sitting in the day room. Gone were the crocheted afghans, the throw rugs, and the Parole Pal dolls. Rules had changed, and officials now wanted to emphasize that these women were not to "nest" here. The authorities wanted the Death Row inmates to realize this was a temporary place for them. All that lay ahead was death. The cell where Karla had lived for so many years stood empty.

I had talked to the women about Terry, so it was wonderful for me to see them all together. They were eager for any word about Karla. Frances, still looking for a miracle, asked, "How did the interview go?"

Frances is beautiful, with high cheekbones and expressive, peaceful dark eyes. She often wears her hair pulled back into a bun, accentuating her sculptured features. She and Karla had walked and prayed together daily, creating a figure-eight path in the exercise area outside Death Row. During these intimate times of sharing heart to heart, God knit their souls together.

After we sat down, I asked Frances to tell Terry about the early years of her relationship with Karla.

"I arrived on November 17, 1988, the day before her birthday," Frances said. "As I walked into my cell, I saw shampoo, deodorant, a writing tablet, and cigarettes lying on my bed waiting for me. Karla and Pam had purchased them at the commissary from their small personal accounts to welcome me to the unit. I hadn't known what to expect and was surprised at their gifts.

"I turned around to thank them, and Pam asked, 'Do you smoke?' That was back before the no-smoking policy started. I told her I didn't. She laughed and said, 'Well, then, give me my cigarettes back!'

"After I got settled, we started talking. When they realized I was athletic like Karla, Pam said, 'You're her birthday present! She's finally got a buddy to play with!'"

Frances stopped a moment as tears slid slowly down her cheek. We waited until she could begin again. She went on to describe a turning point in their relationship

It was her second Christmas on Death Row, but she still felt like an outsider. The women had begun a tradition of making personal items to give to each other at Christmas. Unsure of herself, Frances purchased her gifts from the commissary.

As a surprise, Karla made personalized dolls for each woman. Christmas morning, Frances watched the others open their dolls, amazed at how Karla had matched the hair color, eyes, and even skin tones of the dolls with their owners. *I'll probably get a doll with light skin and long hair, but I'll still appreciate it,* she thought as she slowly unwrapped her present.

"I pulled back the paper and uncovered a beautiful black doll with big brown eyes and short black hair. And then I knew: Karla saw and accepted me for who I am. That made all the difference in our friendship."

We talked about a recent interview when Karla said, "I have some very true friendships on the Row. That's not a normal thing in prison. It's a rare thing to develop a true friendship with somebody in here, but with God that isn't an abnormal thing at all.

"We are here for each other, just to love on. We don't condemn or judge—when we go through stressful times with our cases or the system, we realize it's just normal. We pray together and lift each other up. Sometimes ministering happens when one of us lets the other one cry, or listens without even saying a word—just letting her express what she is going through."

Pam had assumed she'd be the first to be executed. She looked at me, her eyes luminous with tears, and whispered so softly I had to lean closer, "I'm the one who was supposed to be first. I wish I could take her place." She then read a letter from Karla that challenged her to stay focused:

> Trust your Abba Father, Pam, to take care of me.
> Let Him give you peace even though you miss me.
> Use this time to witness for His glory. Let people
> know He is merciful and forgives us. He died on the
> cross, and death can't touch us or sting us! Praise God!

Sis, this is *not* the end. Hang on to hope and the reality that this is only a temporary place. We have a home, not made by human hands! Hallelujah! So, if we go from here or from wherever, it's up to God. We know where we're going! Amen.

Pamie, please let any anger or malice you hold onto go. Let it go. Do not take up offense. Do not get upset with people for things said or how someone believes. We can call right right, wrong wrong, darkness darkness, and evil evil. But call it with a pure heart and give it to God immediately! Let God deal with people. They will be held just as accountable for their beliefs and words as you will for how you react to them. Jesus said pray for them and do good to them.

Girl, the world is watching to see if we are for real and if the God we profess is making a difference in our lives.

As Pam folded her letter and put it back in the envelope, I said, "Karla's exhorting all of us. As I was leaving today she reminded me, 'Linda, don't be sad. I know where I'm going. He's going to be right there on the table with me. He will take me home on His arm.'"

Our time together was ending. We formed a prayer circle—a grandmother from Wisconsin, a television personality from Virginia, and women-in-white. All one heart, all blood-bought, and all forgiven.

◆ ◆ ◆

Walking out into the clear starlit night, Terry thanked

God that I had the privilege of walking this journey. Often, in spite of the pain, I, too, would stand in awe that I was chosen. As we drove away, I decided to show her the view from the hill overlooking the prisons. We turned right and continued up a steep hill to a little Baptist church, and drove into the parking lot. The prison lights stretched across the stark Texas landscape in the valley below. "Terry, I see those lights from my room at the Wises'. Fourteen thousand men and women are housed behind those prison walls. Karla keeps challenging me to go to them." It was more than a challenge from Karla. For years, as Dallas and I drove by the five prisons that stood side by side on Ransom Road, I'd say, "We need to get into these other units." In order for a ministry team to go into prisons, the chaplain in each unit must approve the organization and clear it with the warden. Then the team must send information on every volunteer—social security number, driver's license number, and birth date—to the chaplain.

That evening Terry said, "Linny, let's go past all fourteen prison units. We'll ask God to open prison doors."

We drove slowly past each one. On the left was Hill Top, a woman's prison. A tall, white-brick facility, it sat on top of a hill, surrounded by guard towers and chain-link fences topped with razor wire. As we passed by, we repeated Jesus' words: "I was in prison and you visited me." Then we prayed, "Jesus, it's all up to You. We're available. Show us the way." We drove on toward Riverside, another women's unit, on our right. Six red-brick buildings stood within the barbed-wire compound. We repeated our prayer.

Then we saw, set back from the road, the lights of the prison's drug and alcohol rehabilitation center, Hackberry. Next to it was Valley Unit, where elderly or sick inmates are incarcerated. We again repeated Christ's words. And again we said our prayer.

Over the past ten years we'd watched God develop a ministry team as diverse as the gatherings in the Mountain View chapel: Different nationalities, economic backgrounds, and interests, but with the one common denominator that was the prerequisite for ministry—a love for God and a love for His people.

Later that week I walked into the Isolation Unit wondering where Karla was. A guard asked me to sit down, then said, "She'll be back in a moment."

A few moments later, Karla walked out of a small room with the warden. I could tell she had been crying. Before she entered the unit, I heard her say, "Warden Baggett, it looks like we're going to grow old together."

She slowly walked toward me, pulled up her chair and sat down. "I just agreed to sign the papers agreeing that if my sentence was commuted, I would waive the possibility of parole." I saw how torn she was. "It was so hard for me, but Dana helped. He said, 'We always choose life over death.'"

Chapter Eleven

I'll Meet You
at the Gate

*I eagerly expect and hope that I will in no way be ashamed,
but will have sufficient courage so that now as always
Christ will be exalted in my body, whether by life or by
death. For to me, to live is Christ and to die is gain.*

—*Philippians 1:20-21*

The sun came up on time on February 1, 1998, but
the gray pall covering our hearts obscured the Texas
sunshine. On our drive from Gatesville to Mountain
View we traveled through the now-familiar broad-
shouldered, rolling landscape laid down like a quilt by
God Himself. We sped past the earth-tone prisons
spread out on both sides of the road without really noticing them. Nor were we thinking about the loneliness and
sadness we'd come to know existed inside them. Instead,
our hearts were held captive by the events surrounding
one woman inside Mountain View and the thoughts of
our last visit together. Today's ride felt like the end of a
very long journey, a journey we didn't want to end.

We came to our last turn, Ransom Road, and once
again I noticed the three telephone poles on the distant

Karla looking out of the Death Row unit.

hilltop behind the prison, clumped together like the crosses on Calvary. It was as if God had spoken of this time in symbols—the crosses and the name of the road—long before we began coming here. As permanent fixtures on the prison grounds, the crosses were a visual demonstration of His sovereignty.

Being familiar with the prison's security routines, we thought we knew what to expect, but today was different. Across the road, camera crews, just part of the international media frenzy focusing on this historic event, stood ready to capture up-to-the-moment footage for their next news feed. The *Houston Chronicle*'s Sunday paper described the attention Karla's case was drawing. "From Amsterdam to Zurich, across western Europe, North America, South America and parts of Asia, Karla Faye Tucker . . . has become something short of a household name. . . . Her case has made news in publications as far-flung as the *South China Morning Post,* the *Irish Times*, the *Straits Times* in Singapore, the *Calgary Herald* in Canada. She's made headlines, too, in such Dutch publications as *Dagblad de Limburger* and *Eindhovens Dagblad*. In Germany, she's been fodder for readers of *Sueddeutsche Zeitung* in Munich and the nationally circulated weekly *Die Woche,* as well as other newspapers. In Italy—where anti–death penalty statements are, perhaps, the strongest in Europe—Tucker has not only made headlines, but abolitionists have held rallies to her cause in Rome."

When the cue came from Huntsville, Karla would be transferred there under heavy guard for the execution.

Crowds were already gathering in Huntsville—some waiting to jeer, others to pray.

As we passed the camera crews, I whispered to Dallas, "How can the sun be shining? How can nothing be changed when this painful event is about to take place?"

At the entrance to the prison, we saw the newly erected, temporary guard house. Two guards slowly, mechanically approached our car.

"State your business," said the one closest to us.

Dallas handed him our driver's licenses. "We're here to see Tucker." Clipboard in hand, the guard checked the list and, with an impersonal nod, motioned us through.

I glanced again at Dallas, saw his eyes, and wondered, *Is my husband, so strong and silent through many troubles, about to break apart? Will I, too, be struck by a forty-foot wave of grief?*

We clung to the mercy and grace of a faithful God. The One who had shown Himself faithful, often miraculously so, throughout twenty-seven years of co-laboring with Him. Today would be no different. He assigned this day. He prepared us for just such a time—building our trust in Him and compassion for others through years of ministry in prisons and to those living under self-imposed "death sentences" on the outside. Relaxing in my seat, I silently thanked Him.

After we checked in at the mesh-enclosed guard station, we walked out onto the prison grounds. In front of us, across an expansive green lawn, was the administration building, with the chapel beside it. To our right stood the multipurpose center, which held the Isolation Unit.

We turned right and walked under the narrow breezeway to the steel door. From the other side we heard the jangling of the guard's keys as she unlocked the door. When our eyes met, I saw a pain and compassion not usually visible in guards working in a woman's maximum-security unit.

We walked down the corridor past offices on either side to the area inmates called "the nurse's room," since this unit also held psychiatric patients. A long counter, the guards' station, ran across the back of the area. On either side, two mesh gates separated us from the isolation cells.

I smiled as the guard announced, "Tucker, your spiritual advisors are here." *Spiritual advisors? No,* I thought. *Karla and I are fellow pilgrims on a journey.*

Dallas and I pulled two metal chairs close together in front of the mesh crash gate that opened to the corridor of cells. We could not enter that area. Instead, the guard opened the door and went to get Karla, who would sit on the other side of the gate. We were going to spend two hours together before Chaplain Nelson came to join us. Our last visit would end with communion.

I saw pain and grief on Dallas's face as we waited. I'd seen that same expression when one of our sons was in pain. He loved Karla like his own daughter, and he could do nothing to stop her execution. His sadness seemed unbearable. He looked at me and said, "How did we ever get into this?" Then the tightness in his jaw slowly disappeared. "Yet I wouldn't miss being here for anything. In spite of how much this hurts, it's such a privilege."

The door opened and we watched as Karla walked

toward us with her Bible in hand. She looked tired, drawn, serious. She was dressed, as always, in the white cotton blouse and slacks. Her long, dark, curly brown hair was pulled back with barrettes.

Each time we had met in the last three weeks I struggled to maintain balance. I didn't want to cause her one moment of worry or concern over my grief. I felt like I was in a fishbowl, with the guards and others observing me. When I was with her, part of me wanted to sob, while the other part wanted to spare her, to be a support, to live up to the title "spiritual advisor." Yet it was hard to remain in one particular role: I was her friend, I cared for her as a mother would, and I was her spiritual advisor. All I knew was that I loved her with everything in me, and I wanted her to know that.

"How are the girls doing?" she asked.

I knew how much she missed them. And she knew I shared her love and concern for them. We told her a bit about our most recent visit and then began talking about February 3. We asked her, "What can we do for you?"

"Rather than coming to Huntsville with me," she answered, "I want you to be here at Mountain View. Be with them—Pam, Frances, and the others. They need you.

"Linda, if God calls me home, I know you will be there for Pam and Frances. We all know that the world is watching us, and the world needs to see that there is joy in this as well as pain. There is a pain from loss, a selfish kind of pain, and then it is a wonderful gain, too. You know that I'm going home to be with the Lord, so I'm trusting in your hands to carry that message of joy to the world for me."

During our visits, she said this same thing in a variety of ways three separate times. Each time she would wait for my response. It was as if Karla were commissioning me. Never was she as passionate and zealous as when she encouraged me to tell others the message of the joy she experienced right up to her execution.

As we talked about what she wanted to accomplish, Dallas leaned forward and said, "During one of David's battles with Israel's enemies, he and his men were hiding in a cave while the Philistines were garrisoned at Bethlehem. He became very thirsty and thought about the water from his hometown well, now under control of his enemy.

"One night he cried out, 'Oh, that someone would get me a drink of water from the well near the gate of Bethlehem.' After hearing his cry, three of his men left the cave, broke through the enemy's lines, and brought back the longed-for water. Awed at the extent of their love and concern for him—at their willingness to even sacrifice their lives on his behalf—he refused to drink it. Instead, he poured it out as a sacrifice of thanksgiving.

"Karla, you're like that drink offering—A precious sacrifice for others who are in prison. Your life is already being poured out. We can see that."

Dallas's words were confirmation to her. In a letter to Pam dated January 2, 1998, Karla wrote:

> Pam, what God is doing in my situation is for many, many, many lives. If it goes through it's because God will be able to save you and others through it happening to me. I was asked by a reporter why I thought

I was different, and why it shouldn't happen to me if I truly believed there were other inmates just as devoted to Christ as I am.

I said, "May it begin with me, and if it doesn't, may my situation cause people to stop and think and then let it begin with the one who will come after me." People have a real face now. Perhaps if they see me they'll see everyone and know that Jesus is in these prisons.

During the next moments, as we shared memories, we felt the pain of the coming separation. With tears flooding his well-worn face, Dallas laughingly said, "Karla, you are really hard on my sinuses."

Not missing a beat, she replied with a playful smile, "You'll get no sympathy from me."

Dallas was returning to Wisconsin later that day. With a heavy heart and a commitment to fast and pray, he said, "Karla, if you get your pardon, I'm blowing the shofar!" (A shofar, a ram's horn, is used in Israel as a call to battle or a call to worship. In Karla's case, it was to be a call to worship.)

"Promise to blow the shofar whether I get the pardon or go home," Karla responded.

I realized that our last two hours were coming to an end when I heard the officer's keys jangling and the door to the Isolation Unit clang shut. Chaplain Nelson entered, talking quietly with the guard as he approached us. As he passed by, he touched our shoulders. He then went with the guard into the cellblock where Karla was sitting, alone, behind the diamond-shaped mesh. Relief filled my heart. She now had this gentle, godly man sitting next to her. *Please God, don't let me miss these precious moments,* I prayed.

Looking somber, he began by saying, "Let's lay aside any preconceived ideas about taking communion. Instead let's focus on the truth that because of His body and blood we are one with Christ."

With the thought of Karla's death looming in the background, I felt like we were in the upper room of long ago as Jesus prepared the disciples for His death. They didn't understand the implications of His death and they didn't want Him to leave them. Likewise, I didn't understand why Karla had to die and I didn't want her to leave me.

On one of my restless nights I had opened my Bible and read Revelation 19:1,7-9: "Hallelujah! Salvation and glory and power belong to our God. . . . Let us rejoice and be glad and give him glory. For the wedding of the Lamb has come, and his bride has made herself ready. Fine linen, bright and clean, was given her to wear. . . . Blessed are those who are invited to the wedding supper of the Lamb!" I also read Psalm 34:5: "Those who look to him are radiant; their faces are never covered with shame."

In my final visits, I noticed a bridal radiance about Karla that far outweighed her weariness. A bride walking down the aisle has a single focus: to be with her bridegroom. I saw that same eagerness in Karla, almost as if she wanted to run down the aisle to be with Christ. The joy and anticipation of what her life would be with her beloved Jesus transformed her appearance. In all she said, in all she did, I witnessed an increasing intimacy between the Bridegroom and Karla—and knew I was losing her. She was going to Him.

As we began the communion service she asked, "Can we sing 'Were You There When They Crucified My Lord?' But I don't want to sing the first verse, just the one that says, 'Were you there when He rose up from the grave?'" Her focus was on the power and reality of the resurrection.

We sang together softly. None of us could sing well, but that didn't matter. Not now, in these moments of quiet tears and gentle love. This cellblock was usually so noisy, but there was a reverence as we sang.

After we broke bread, we began drinking from the cup, and I felt overwhelmed by the awesome work of Calvary. The blood of Jesus. His blood, shed for wounded, broken, sinful people. His blood, shed for a woman known as a pickax murderer. His blood shed for me. *O, Abba Father, how great the price of her redemption—and ours—which we cannot fully realize with our finite minds.*

Karla began to softly sing "Thou Art Worthy," one of her favorite praise choruses. "Thou art worthy, thou art worthy, O Lord, to receive glory, honor, and power. . . ."

I could not join her. My spirit agreed with her, but the words wouldn't come out. The sorrow of the consequences of her sin—her death by lethal injection—consumed me.

As our visit was ending, I said, "Karla, Jacob memorized Psalm 23:4 in kindergarten this week: 'Even though I walk through the valley of the shadow of death,

I will fear no evil, for you are with me; your rod and your staff, they comfort me.' Jake knows why I have been traveling back and forth to Texas, and we've been talking about what it means to die and go to heaven. One day he said, 'Grandma, your hands are so wrinkled, like great-grandma's. Are you going to die?' His question hung in the air for a moment, as if he were contemplating all that this meant. 'I don't want you to die, Grandma,' he said, his big brown eyes fixed intently on me to see just how I was going to answer his question.

"I had smiled at him and said, 'Well, Jake, I don't have any immediate plans, but one day I will die. And when I do, I'm going to heaven to be with Jesus forever!'

"'Well, Grandma, will you please wait for me at the gate?'

"'Yes, Jake, I'll be there, waiting at the gate for you.'"

I told Karla, "The Shepherd is here, Karla, and He's going all the way home with you. Wait for me at the gate. I'll be there in fifteen minutes."

Karla smiled and nodded, then turned her focus on us. Returning to the words of the twenty-third Psalm she said, "He will lead you beside still waters. Remember to drink. The next two days will be very difficult. Drink."

I'd never realized the value of still, quiet water as I did that day when I felt so weary and dry, so in need of comfort. Time was up. Tears flowed unashamedly. We pressed our cheeks to the cold iron mesh, kissed one another, and said, "I love you."

"See you at the gate," I said. Then we turned and slowly walked through the reception area and down the long corridor toward the steel door of the Isolation Unit. I faced straight ahead, knowing my next meeting with Karla would be at the gate.

◆ ◆ ◆

Many who loved Karla so much remember their last contact with her.

Sunday, January 18—Isolation Unit

The day after the rally in Austin, our son Terry walked with us to the multipurpose center. He asked, "Mom and Dad, since I'm going back home today, could I have ten minutes alone with Karla before we leave?"

We agreed, and as our visit drew to a close, we stepped back. Terry moved his chair closer to the crash gate so they could speak privately, their fingers locked between the mesh.

She looked directly at him. "I'm so proud of you and Jean, for the way you are raising little Jacob. I love the picture you sent where he was wearing the slippers I made and signed, 'I love you.' I could tell he wasn't ashamed to be wearing them. I'm proud of the way you're instilling the heart of God in him. I'm proud of the way you've surrendered to the Lord. You come in here and let God use you. You are open to everything He is doing."

Like Paul with Timothy, and Moses with Joshua, she was passing on the baton. She knew she was going to die and was encouraging him to run the race, to finish the work. "You're needed on the team, Terry. Don't forget about the men in prison. There are over 450 men on Death Row in Huntsville."

Choking back tears, he promised, "I won't, Karla."

There was a moment of silence and then she said, "I'll be up there with that great cloud of witnesses, Terry, cheering you on." Then she quoted Hebrews 12:1. "Therefore, since we are surrounded by such a great cloud of witnesses, let us throw off everything that hinders and the sin that so easily entangles, and let us run with perseverance the race marked out for us."

Before he left, Terry said hesitantly, "Karla, would you pray for me? I want to have that same relationship with Christ that you have."

Bowing their heads, their fingers still linked, she prayed what felt like a benediction and then they said their good-byes. He didn't even try to hold back his tears. Still facing Karla, he stood up and walked backward from the gate before finally turning to join us. We hugged and then the three of us walked toward the door. He turned one last time to wave good-bye to the woman Jesus had used in his life as a demonstration of His life-changing, personal love.

Thursday, January 29, 1998—River Hills, Wisconsin

I had been teaching a weekly Bible study for twenty years. Today people from the study and others on the ministry team gathered at Mayflower Church in River Hills as J.J. videotaped them. Karla had wanted to express her love to the ministry team with the tape she had made, and now we were expressing our love back to her. Everyone on the team wanted to be with her in Texas. They couldn't, but they could send their love on videotape.

Dallas brought the tape to Gatesville with him. After Warden Baggett and Chaplain Nelson reviewed it, Karla watched it late in the evening on January 31, 1998, the night before our final visit and communion service.

End of January 1998—Mountain View Unit

Lieutenant Woody escorted Pam and Frances to the visiting room. Pam described their last visit: "We were told that the only way we could visit was if we didn't cry, talk about death, or show any emotion. So, of course, we cried, talked about death, and showed emotion. I wanted to protect her. I felt so helpless. She was like my sister. I wanted to tell Karla how much I would miss her. She was very upbeat. I knew she had peace, but my heart was broken. I didn't know then that I would see Karla one more time."

That final glimpse would come on Saturday, January 31. "My son and mom were visiting me the Saturday before her execution. As I walked in, I saw Karla sitting in the first security cage talking with her attorneys, Mac Secrest and David Botsford. I knew I couldn't talk to her. The guard took me to the first chair on the opposite end of the room, then went to bring my mom and Joseph in from the other side of the wall. While I waited, I glanced at Karla. As my family walked in, I heard the guard instruct them not to talk to Karla.

"My mom said, 'You mean I can't say good-bye?'

"'No, ma'am. Sorry, but those are the rules during a situation like this.'

"I saw the look on my mom's face as she continued, 'But I've known Karla for fourteen years. You mean I can't say good-bye or I love you?'

"'Ma'am, I understand what you're feeling, but I have rules to go by here.'

"My mom and son sat down and we talked for a while. All three of us could hardly speak without crying. Joseph finally said he was going to go get a soda for me. He walked out to the soda machine and when he came back, he went to where the guard was sitting behind the wire mesh next to the security cage. As he gave the soda to the guard to give to me, Karla gently said, 'I love you, Joseph.'

"'I love you, too,' he said, and their eyes met. But he knew the rules, so he slowly walked away."

Saturday, January 31, 1998, 6:45 A.M.—Mountain View Unit

In a letter, Fran Turner described her last time with Karla:

> Karla and I hadn't seen each other since the officers walked with her past the beauty shop en route to the visiting room for her last interview. Following standard procedures, two officers always escorted her, with her hands cuffed behind her. One walked next to her with one hand on top of her cuffed arms, the other guard carried a bully stick. One of the guards who often escorted Karla,

Mr. Harris, has a kind, gentle spirit and loves the Lord. He shows respect to us and never makes us feel less than a lady. Karla was so fond of him.

The last time I saw her, I kept assuring her that the governor could spare her life.

"Frannie, this isn't in the governor's hands. It's in God's."

We talked about all the letters she'd received. That was troubling her, the fact that she didn't have time to read or answer them all. She told me how much she loved me, that she would see me on the other side, and that she'd watch for me.

I cried out, "Hush!" I didn't want to hear that.

"Are you afraid, Karla?"

"No, not fearful. Just anxious."

She'd been fasting and looked frail. We talked for about fifteen minutes, knowing we'd never see each other again in this world. I knew our time together was short, and I didn't want to leave, and I began crying. She asked me not to be sad and said, "I'm not sad. In fact I'm excited about seeing Jesus face to face."

That's when the guard came back and said, "It's time to go, Fran."

Karla signed "I love you," kissed the glass, and smiled real big. I stepped away and broke down crying.

Early morning February 2, 1998—Death Row, Gatesville Unit

Before dawn on February 2, Karla Faye Tucker, inmate 777, was escorted by her friend and warden, Pamela

Baggett, to a waiting van with tinted windows. Even at that early hour, security measures were tight. Karla's famous, long, curly, dark hair was tucked into her prison jacket. Officer Harris drove her past Death Row, the place she had called home for the past fourteen years.

Frances, unable to sleep, was up early and saw shadows going past. Running to the window, cupping her eyes with her hands, she pressed her face against the frosted pane.

"That's her," she whispered.

Top: Karla in the multipurpose room on Death Row
at Christmas.
Bottom: Frances, Karla, and Pam: Cellmates, friends,
and prayer partners.

Chapter Twelve

The Light in the Chapel

Precious in the sight of the LORD is the death of his saints.

— *Psalm 116:15*

*I want those who are left behind if February 3rd does hap-
pen to have a peace. We pray and we believe God is going
to do it our way. But if His way is to call me home, we have
to accept that, and we have to have peace with that too.*

—*Karla Faye Tucker, January 17, 1998*

Monday, February 2—Huntsville

On February 2, sixteen of the eighteen members of the
Texas Board of Pardons and Paroles voted to deny
Karla's request for clemency; two abstained.

Karla's concern for those in prison was displayed before the world up to the moment of her execution. A *San
Antonio Express-News* article dated February 4, 1998,
describes an encounter between Allan Polunsky, chairman of the Texas Board of Criminal Justice, and Karla in
Huntsville's Goree Unit, on Monday, February 2, at
7:30 P.M. (Polunsky saw Karla three times during her

last twenty-four hours.) Karla's cell was sparse, with just a small bed, so she sat on the floor during their conversation. Although a guard offered a chair, Polunsky declined, choosing to sit on the floor opposite her cell door. "Otherwise," he said later, "I would have been talking down to her."

He described their conversation as "very respectful, very cordial. She was remarkably upbeat and hopeful that her appeals would succeed or that the governor would intervene, but she was ready for execution if her lawyers were unsuccessful."

During their hour together, she presented him with a three-page letter encouraging the system to do more to reach inmates. She asked the Prison Board to expand programs to help her fellow inmates and suggested that the system needed to be more aggressive in making inmates responsible for their actions—inside the system and in the free world. She also encouraged them to add additional training programs and pay inmates for their labor. Her goal, in paying inmates, was to teach them fiscal responsibility. Part of the money would recover costs of their incarceration.

Tuesday, February 3, 8:00 A.M.—Gatesville

The weather in Texas was marvelous as Mary Stocking and I entered the chapel. True to her promise several years earlier, she was walking with me through this journey.

"I'm so grateful for this place of refuge, especially today," I said as we walked through the narthex to the chaplain's office. We knew Chaplain Nelson was in Huntsville, ministering to Karla's family at the Hospitality House. During the final days leading up to an execution, inmates' family and friends can stay there at no charge. The Hospitality House, a place of comfort for people in need, is similar in concept to Ronald McDonald Houses, which are located close to hospitals. Today we would coordinate our assignment with Andy Andreason. Andy was a volunteer chaplain at the prison, a retired assistant commissioner for administration with the IRS, and the president of Texas Baptist Men.

Six hundred women live in the Mountain View Unit, and, per Karla's last request, we were visiting the individual cellblocks. Being an evangelist at heart, my assignment of going cell to cell was the greatest gift Karla could have given me that day. It kept me focused as I saw the love of God coming into barren areas.

Andy, a tall, broad-shouldered, ex-military man, sat behind Chaplain Nelson's desk. When we entered, he got up, and with obvious concern asked, "How are you doing this morning? The chapel will be open this evening for women who want to come and pray before the execution." Then he looked directly at me. "Would you be willing to lead them in prayer and be available to the women?" He waited for my acceptance.

I didn't know how to respond. I felt a tension between my commitment to the women on Death Row and the needs of others. Conflicting thoughts tugged at my heart, but I knew what the Lord wanted. I told Andy yes.

Sensing my hesitation, he assured me I could go to Death Row after the service. Then he went on to say,

"We received all the clearance we need for you to go to segregation, the cellblocks, and housing units." He seemed eager to send us out.

We were eager too; it was a mission we knew we were called to. Yet we also knew it was impossible to reach all the inmates. The Lord would have to lead us to the ones He had prepared.

As we talked, Carole Ross, a volunteer chaplain and former guard, joined us. Our first stop would be the Segregation Unit (Seg), the section of the prison where inmates are sent as a result of discipline problems. Either they are a threat to the physical safety of staff members, other inmates, or themselves, or they are an escape risk.

"Are you prepared for what you could experience in Seg?" Carole asked. We'd been there before and knew that it was a lonely, boring, yet scary place to live. The women, some who do not speak English, are not permitted to leave their cells except for the state-required hour of daily exercise or to shower. Inmates typically feel like outcasts from society anyway, so these women were the least of the least in the prison system, the outcasts of the outcasts. That's where Jesus would want us to go.

As we walked into the unit I heard the loud outbursts of angry women. Swearing. Yelling back and forth at one another. The guards looked at us as if we were crazy to be there. One guard was escorting a handcuffed inmate to an enclosed corner room.

Carole explained what was happening. "These inmates often violate the posted TDC written policies and procedures, such as creating a disturbance or destroying state property. Each time they do, they receive a ticket.

Since this is an official disciplinary action, they have to come before a committee, made up of the assistant warden and a guard who is at least the rank of a captain or above. When they appear before the committee, the inmates are provided a substitute counsel since a disciplinary action can add time onto their Seg sentence. That happens a lot with this population. Some women have been here for two to six years."

As we walked down one of the two separate corridors, a few women deliberately turned their backs on us to let us know we were unwelcome intruders. One woman glared at us, defying us to comment. But most were not belligerent. Staring warily at us with eyes that spoke volumes of anguish, fear, and hopelessness, they waited to see why we were there.

Although momentarily stunned by the commotion, I felt called to announce our mission. I knew the importance and seriousness of this day and I was free from inhibitions. I stretched out my hands and yelled, "I'm here with a message from Karla Faye Tucker. You know her execution is scheduled for 6:00 P.M. tonight. That's when she will leave the gurney and be with Jesus. It is her desire for you to have the peace that she has. We are going to walk from cell to cell. If you want to talk, come over to the bars."

Carole suggested, "I will go to the end of the unit and work back. You and Mary can start here."

We began walking down the cold cement corridor between the cells. As we passed by we heard one of the ladies say, "Sh—!"

Mary immediately turned to her cell, smiled, and said,

"That's one of my favorite words—and I'm trying hard not to say it."

Intrigued, the woman came forward to talk to her. I knew Mary had found where she belonged, so I left her there and continued walking. One woman called out to me, "Hey, come on over here. Talk with me a minute. Is this Karla for real? I mean, do you really believe she's not scared?"

I walked over to her cell and grabbed the steel bars, giving her my full attention. I could see the woman in the next cell sitting on her cot. She was obviously irritated, muttering words I was glad I could not understand.

I began by telling the first woman what I had seen and heard from being with Karla, knowing that first-hand accounts of events are the most powerful. As I did so, the second woman nonchalantly walked over and said flatly, "I stabbed a lady with scissors sixteen times. I'm in for capital murder. If there is a God, then why am I living and this woman is going to be executed?"

This was her challenge, but it wasn't my battle. It was God's. I admitted that to her. "I don't have answers to all the questions, but I know that I've seen God's presence in this situation. And it isn't about that anyway. That's not why I'm here. I'm here because Karla wants you to know what she knows.

"Look at where you're at." I spread my arms out to indicate the steel bars and the confusion around us. "There's got to be more than this." I could not keep from weeping as I said these words. At the sight of my tears, she began to soften. Now tears welled up in her eyes. After talking for several more moments, I began to see a remorse in her that could only be explained as a work of the Holy Spirit.

The first woman looked at me in amazement. "I have never seen her cry before. She *doesn't* cry!"

Realizing that this was her moment in time, I asked this wounded, broken woman to pray with me. I knelt on the cold cement floor, face to face with a woman whose appearance was being changed before my eyes. I can't say that I can return to that unit today and see this woman living out her faith. The spiritual battle is intense where women with lifelong problems are locked up twenty-four hours a day with other women who have equally difficult backgrounds. What I do know is that at that moment this woman encountered the living God— and I did too.

3:30 P.M.—*Huntsville*

Cheryl Archer, the women's staff chaplain who had become Karla's friend, slowly opened the door as she left the Hospitality House. After taking a deep breath to quell the rising emotion, she purposely looked straight ahead, past the crush of protesters and camera crews between her and the goal: her last visit with Karla.

As she walked toward the gate to the Walls Unit, Karla's attorney David Botsford handed her a note. "Please read this to Karla," he whispered. The reporters, recognizing him, instantly thrust a dozen microphones in Cheryl's face. Later, she said, "I glanced down at a rosé-bordered piece of note paper and put it in my pocket."

She pressed her way through the crowd, walked up to

the gate, and handed her badge to the officers. Following a "pat search," Cheryl and the guards headed down a narrow walkway between thick cement walls that towered twenty feet into the air. "I felt claustrophobic as we wound through the bowels of the prison," she said. "I was lost in thought as the guards silently escorted me. I was saying farewell to a true friend.

"After a long walk through a narrow maze, a lieutenant opened heavy double doors. I saw her standing outside a small, barren cell. She smiled as I walked over, and for an instant we held hands. Then Karla quickly released my hands and stepped back inside her cell. The officers were visibly shaken by her willingness to comply with the system's rules without needing to be told. Just as quickly, they locked her door.

"Karla and I sat on the floor, our legs crossed under us. The steel mesh separating us was too thick for our fingers to touch, so we leaned forward, our foreheads resting on the mesh. I tried not to cry.

"When I could finally talk, I took the folded paper from my pocket. 'David slipped me this on the way over and asked me to read it.'

"I read the note aloud: 'Karla, the Fifth Circuit denied at 2:45. So last chance in Supreme Court hearing in Austin is ongoing to declare Board's votes illegal to force reprieve. Al Gonzales called from governor's office. He will call again. I love you and will be with you in heart, spirit, and the Lord. Botsford.'

"Karla looked down momentarily, but quickly raised her head, her brown eyes gazing compassionately into mine. She had a way of looking deep into your heart, while her eyes searched your face, wanting to make sure you were okay. She smiled for an instant and said, 'You know I'm at peace with this, Cheryl. I want you to make sure the women don't hold this against the system. Tell them to forgive.'

"Our time together was brief, maybe twenty or thirty minutes. She began praying as I choked back tears. She looked fragile and I wanted to rescue her. I couldn't stop the next two hours, yet I couldn't imagine her no longer being a part of my life. As we prayed, Karla's prayers were for her family, friends, and, of course, Dana. One of the last things she said was, 'Cheryl, encourage Dana to marry again. This has been an incredibly long journey for him, and I want him to be happy.'

"I don't remember getting up from the cold cement floor or leaving. I felt numb. I barely remember the long walk out of the dark prison. But I clearly remember stepping out and seeing the angry, jeering crowd and hearing the familiar, unforgettable sounds of 'Amazing Grace' [coming from the stage set up by the church that had ministered to Karla]. The contrast was jarring. I felt like I was walking through the crowd at the crucifixion.

"As I entered the Hospitality House, David Botsford was on the phone pleading to talk to Governor Bush. He was denied. He hung up the phone, and we all began waiting for what was now inevitable."

Austin, State Capitol

At 5:00 P.M., Al Gonzales [Secretary of State of Texas and formerly general counsel] called Karla Faye

Tucker's lawyer, David Botsford, to ask about the Supreme Court's decision. Once again, the Supreme Court had denied his request to halt her execution, but Mr. Botsford said he was on his way to file more appeals with the court of criminal appeals in Texas. Thirty or forty minutes that seemed like three or four hours later, we learned that the Texas court had denied the requests. At that moment, the phone rang. It was the lawyer, Mr. Botsford, calling to let Al know that he had run out of venues and would not be filing any more pleadings in court. After reviewing all the facts one final time, I made up my mind.

—*George W. Bush,* A Charge to Keep
(*William Morrow, 1999*)

At 6:12 P.M. Bush decided against granting a 30-day reprieve to Tucker, clearing the way for her execution in Huntsville. . . .

Earlier in the day, the U. S. Supreme Court rejected three challenges to Tucker's death sentence under criminal and federal civil rights laws. There was no dissent and no comment by the justices.

In addition, the 5th U. S. Circuit Court of Appeals in New Orleans turned away her attorneys' efforts to start another round of federal challenges. State courts also rejected her contention that the Texas Board of Pardons and Paroles violated the state's Open Meetings Act by not holding a public hearing or public vote in her clemency appeal.

—Houston Chronicle, *February 4, 1998*

Huntsville

Shortly after 1 P.M. Tucker was moved to a holding cell near the prison's execution chamber. For her last meal she ordered a light vegetarian meal: a banana, a peach, and a tossed salad.

Tucker refused breakfast, eating some crackers only at the urging of her husband, Dana Brown, after Tucker appeared weak during her last family visit. A prison spokesman said Tucker wanted to continue a fast she began some days ago.

Tucker's four-hour meeting with her husband, whom she married while in prison, and her father and sister ended at noon. "She remained fairly upbeat until the time her visit ended," the prison spokesman said. He called the parting "emotional."

—USA Today, *February 4, 1998*

On her last day, Tucker spent her time writing a letter and visiting with Brown; her sister, Kari Weeks; and father, Lawrence Tucker. She cried briefly at one point in the morning.

Tucker and her husband have not consummated their marriage. They weren't allowed any contact on her final day either.

She and her family, however, pressed their hands together on the heavy mesh screen separating them in their final hours. Tucker also read passages from the Bible to them.

—San Antonio Express-News, *February 4, 1998*

Gatesville

From 10:30 to 5:30 P.M. we walked from unit to unit, bringing Karla's message of hope. "Grab onto the hope that Jesus gives. Keep your head up. Pray for His joy, that undergirding joy." As we shared her message, we saw God's love come to these women living in despair. I was so focused on the goal that I hardly thought of where Karla was and what she was doing. I only knew that I was doing what she had called me to do. I thought, *If I keep doing this long enough, this day will never end. I won't have to deal with 6:00 P.M.*

While I knew her attorneys were doing everything possible to stop the execution, I also realized 6:00 P.M. was inevitable. Later that day, I was heading toward the chapel to begin the service when one of the guards called me over to where she was standing with a distraught prisoner. "This woman's on her way to the chapel. Would you walk over with her?"

I put my arm around her and said, "I'm so grateful you've chosen to come to chapel this evening."

As we walked in I felt like I'd hit a brick wall. It was 5:30. No one had intervened. The execution was going to take place. Even though my stomach knotted, I still felt wrapped in God's cocoon of grace. Thirty women were already seated in the paneled sanctuary.

Tammy, the chaplain's assistant, walked toward me. She knew how difficult this day had been and had prayed for me and given me several hugs as we passed during the day. One of my favorite passages of Scripture is Matthew 10:42: "If anyone gives even a cup of cold water to one of these little ones because he is my disciple, I tell you the truth, he will certainly not lose his reward." I thought I was here to give these women a cup of cold water. Instead the women now offered healing to me.

We started the service by singing "Amazing Grace." Stephanie, an inmate who sings like Whitney Houston, came alongside me and helped lead the singing. As the worship progressed, women continued to come in, some weeping. Many slouched down in the pews, as if they'd been running a race and had finally given up. Soon about one hundred inmates were singing and worshipping God.

Then Fran stood and read a letter with a challenge from Karla: "Let the people on the outside know that those of us behind the walls are sure that God is alive today, no matter what happens."

Warden Baggett had assigned extra officers to oversee the service. The staff throughout the prison had been increased on this day because no one knew if the inmates' frustration might erupt in violence. Yet, instead of remaining aloof at the back, the guards began walking throughout the chapel, gently placing their hands on the shoulders of the women who seemed especially broken. I saw several guards wiping tears from their eyes.

Oh, Karla, I thought, *what an impact your life has made on everyone. I wish you could see how the walls are coming down between guards and prisoners tonight.*

Stephanie whispered, "It's 6:00. Let's sing 'The Battle Hymn of the Republic.'"

As we got to the chorus, the women-in-white stood to

their feet and sang, "Glory, glory hallelujah! Glory, glory hallelujah!"

The sight of these women standing there, singing with tears coursing down their cheeks, overwhelmed me. I covered my face with my hands and began to sob. I didn't think I would be able to say anything, much less give these women a word of comfort.

Tammy was immediately by my side with several other inmates. They laid their hands on me, and as they prayed they formed a protective circle of love around me. Tammy said, "God has brought you here for us. He is going to see you through this. You've been given words for us. You go, girl!"

Austin/Huntsville

We sat in my capitol office, waiting, as prison officials led her to the death chamber. We patched the phone line into the general counsel's office, where my deputy counsel, Donna Davidson, quietly repeated the words of the warden as she heard them. "6:25, prisoner led from cell." Joe Allbaugh, my chief of staff, Al Gonzales, Clay Johnson, and I sat there, not moving. "6:26, prisoner strapped to gurney." Karen Hughes [communications director] wandered in and out, periodically leaving to brief the press on the status, then returning, worried, to look at me. I felt like a huge piece of concrete was crushing me as we waited. "6:28, needle inserted." No one said another word. "6:30, lethal dose administered." Finally, what seemed like hours later: "Prisoner is pronounced dead."

—*George W. Bush*, A Charge to Keep

Gatesville

The next forty-five minutes seemed to last forever. Mary kept looking out the window, hoping for some sign that Karla had gone home. Then she heard the still small voice of the Lord say, "Don't look out the window for me, look in the faces of one another."

Suddenly the emergency lights in the chapel came on, lighting up the entire altar area. The cross was illuminated as I'd never seen it before. (No one was ever able to explain why this happened, since the electricity in the prison was still functioning.)

Then I heard the phone ring in the chaplain's office. A moment later Andy came to the altar where I was standing. Slowly he announced, "At 6:45 P.M. Karla Faye Tucker went home to be with her Lord and Savior, Jesus Christ."

As he announced her death some inmates sobbed. Others raised their hands to God. I remember thinking, *Thank You, God. Thank You, Father. Thank You that she's with You. I'm glad it's finally over. She's home at last.*

❖ ❖ ❖

It was 7:30 before we walked across the sidewalk to the chain-link fence leading to Death Row. Keisha, a yellow tiger-striped cat, meowed in the barred window well. She was the last cat on Death Row. Over the years she'd get pregnant, have her kittens, nurse them a little while, then walk away. The women loved the kittens and fed them, becoming surrogate mothers in the process. As I saw Keisha lying there, I thought about a story Fran had recently told me.

"Early one winter morning, Karla and Pam were sitting on the sidewalk in the exercise area during a winter rain holding their cats and crying. Their green trench coats were drenched with icy rain and their hair was soaking wet. They were stroking the cats' backs and praying over them. An officer had been injured by one of the cats—he had to go on disability for a while—and so the warden decided to take action. The cats were to be poisoned.

"Other inmates couldn't bear to see Karla and Pam hurting like that, so they asked visitors and other officers to bring pet carriers to take the cats home. Many cats were saved. Some were still left and ate the poison, but not Keisha."

So far Keisha was the sole survivor. I wondered what would happen to her now. These thoughts quickly left me as the officer opened the gate into the grassy exercise area and escorted us to the steel door. He took a six-inch brass key from his belt, unlocked the door, and motioned for us to enter.

The room was dimly lit by bare bulbs overhead. Park benches were securely bolted to the cement floor. The reality of Karla's death hit me again. She was not running toward me, eager to greet us.

Pam and Frances got up to hug us. Pam's face was red and raw from crying. Warden Moten, a former warden at Mountain View who is now senior warden at the Gatesville units, and Mountain View's Associate Warden Thomas, stood behind the bench like bodyguards. While attentive to their official responsibilities as representatives of the prison system, they stood ready to provide comfort.

For a moment no one spoke. We all stared absently at the television. Tonight the world's focus centered on Huntsville, a city of less than thirty-five thousand people, eighty miles north of Houston. A grim-faced newscaster was describing details of the execution as scenes of the carnival atmosphere in Huntsville filled the screen. The camera zoomed in on a member of the College Republicans of Texas who held aloft a sign showing a dripping hypodermic needle. "Karla Faye Tucker," it said, "This Is Your Last Shot." The camera panned the rowdy crowd at the prison, estimated at over one thousand people, finally focusing on a man dressed like the Grim Reaper, who held an overripe banana, mocking Karla's request for a last meal of fruit and salad. "It's fun. It's history," he said.

This was such a contrast to the way we felt. I looked at Pam and Frances as I said, "On January 15, Karla was thinking of you and prepared a gift she asked me to give you tonight."

I couldn't wait to play that video. I wanted to move beyond the horrendous scenes outside to a place of hope. I knew I couldn't speak, and like so many times when we were without words, it was Karla who spoke the word of hope. Her face appeared on the television, but this time it wasn't from news clips. It was our beloved friend speaking directly to the women beside me.

"I've never wrestled with God about February 3rd. I've always put that in His hands and have a great peace about it. If February 3rd does happen, I want you to have a peace with it too. We pray and we believe God is going to do it our way. But if His way is to call me home, we have to accept that. We have to have peace with that too.

"We have to go on. Just like the believers mentioned in the faith chapter of Hebrews. There were those who died believing. We accept whatever He gives us and use that as a way to minister to others.

"I love you guys. You've been such a big part of my life for so many years. Through you I have learned about friendship and how to be a true friend. I want to thank you for being part of my life. Thank you for allowing me into your hearts. I will see you when you get here."

The women were astonished that Karla had thought to do something so personal for them when she was under such tension. They went from moments of crying and despair to a place of peace. It was as if she were right there with us—and yet we all knew she was with Jesus.

The wardens eventually left, and Mary and I were alone with the two officers on duty, and Pam and Frances. At about 8:30 P.M. Frances asked if we'd like something to eat. I couldn't eat anything. I felt nauseated and exhausted. Mary could see how shaken I was and she immediately suggested that we return to the Wises' home.

Soon after we arrived, the phone rang. It was Mary Alice calling from the Hospitality House in Huntsville. "Linda," she said, her voice trembling. She was speaking so softly, I had to strain to hear her.

"It was awful, like a nightmare."

"I know, Mary Alice. I saw CNN tonight."

"Charlie and I couldn't believe the way the people were. It wasn't just the crude signs. We decided to leave the Hospitality House to walk over to a platform set up for Christians so we could pray with those gathered there. For the first time in my life, I knew what it was like to be in the middle of a mob, and it was chilling.

"As we tried to get through the crowd, we were shoved as the people continued waving their signs, jumping up and down, or running back and forth. We eventually just stopped trying to get to the platform and knelt down. Charlie and I held hands and prayed for Karla and those who were with her. Yet even while we were kneeling we were almost shoved over by the crowd."

By now, we were both crying. We prayed together then and I hung up. A moment later, the phone rang again.

This time it was Dallas. I told him about what had occurred at the prison and about my phone call with Mary Alice. He comforted me and we cried together. Then he said, "Linda, you won't believe this, but at 5:45 the crew from Channel 4 came to our house. They wanted to film my reaction to the execution."

"Oh, no! What did you do?" I asked.

"It took me by surprise, so I let them in. I told them I had promised Karla I'd be on my knees praying as she faced her death. I explained that Terry, Jean, and Jake would be with me in the guest room praying. At 6:00 I took them into our bedroom where the television is, so they could watch the CNN reports while I went back to pray."

"Was the bed made?" I interrupted, surprising myself.

"No, and my suitcase wasn't unpacked, either. At 6:45 they walked into the room with the word that Karla had gone home. Linda, they were filming me as they spoke! And I was crying and Terry was crying. I hope what I said made some sense. I can't begin to describe the pain I felt. But I remembered my promise to Karla. I went to the hearth, took the shofar down, and blew it."

A year later, on February 3, 1999, and again on February 3, 2000, Dallas picked up that same shofar from the mantle of our home and blew it as a reminder that we had moved one year closer to meeting Karla at the gate.

Chapter Thirteen

He Is Risen

They were on their way to the tomb and they asked each other, "Who will roll the stone away from the entrance of the tomb?" But when they looked up, they saw that the stone, which was very large, had been rolled away.

—Mark 16:3-4

Karla was a murderer who said yes to God. She passed every test; she did not stumble once through the most severe trials. She walked with the glory of God upon her, with clarity and joy, never doubting His faithfulness. She used her time in prison to train for her final moments. Every day God put before her life and death. Each time she chose life, and that choice resulted in the joy we saw in her. As she became a stronger Christian, she ministered that strength and joy to anyone who would receive it, always pointing to Him and away from herself.

—Mary Stocking, 1998

On February 4, the day after Karla's execution, Mary and I went back to Death Row. Warden Baggett was already there when we arrived, and her presence assured the women that she understood. I was certain she was

Karla saying goodbye at the close of a seminar. Her cell is behind her.
"I'll meet you at the gate."

exhausted, physically and emotionally. On Monday, February 2, unable to accompany Karla on the plane to Huntsville, she had followed in her car. Now, forty-eight hours later, she was back with us on Death Row.

We all wanted to hear how it had been for Karla. We cried as Warden Baggett described Karla's last moments. "Unable to have a barrette or clip, she'd pulled her hair back, tied it with toilet paper, and even made a bow. She looked so small laying on the gurney. She was very brave, and concerned for all those around her who were hurting. After speaking her last words, she seemed to be humming."

As Warden Baggett talked, we realized again that even to the end Karla did not exhibit self-pity. Not even in her final moments did she display an attitude of "Woe is me." Instead, her attitude was "Glory to God"--and she expected us to behave the same.

Before Warden Baggett left, the women thanked her for taking the time to come and be with them.

Of course, none of the women on Death Row would be able to attend Karla's funeral service. Yet, when someone we loves dies, the sharing of treasured memories is an important step in the grieving process. I couldn't imagine anywhere else I would have wanted to be than with these women she loved so much. Our own personal memorial service started when Mary began to help us give expression to our grief. She had brought a blown-up picture of Karla's face, cut into irregular pieces like a puzzle. "We know what the Bible says about each person's importance in the body of Christ. Well, each of us is a part of Christ's body, and if one piece is missing it's incomplete. Karla's gone home now. None of us can be Karla, but each of us are integral to the whole, to the work that Christ continues to do in and through us."

Mary poured the puzzle pieces out from a large envelope onto the tabletop. "Take a couple," she instructed. Without speaking to each other, we each selected several pieces, holding each one as tenderly as we would something of great worth. We knew the value they represented. Never again would we see Karla's smile, hear her laugh, or pray together. The moment of silence passed and we began spontaneously putting the face together. While we saw the reality of what Mary was saying, on another level, putting the pieces of Karla's face together was very healing, as if were mending something broken.

I thought about Karla's expressive eyes and the way she really saw people. In a letter to Cheryl, Karla had written, "I think of how Jesus sees us now—the completed work, as opposed to how we see ourselves and others." That is how we felt Karla saw us—like Jesus does, fully accepting, flaws and all. She had a special gift of making each of us feel as if we were the most important person in the world to her. It didn't seem to matter whether someone was a television personality, volunteer, or a fellow inmate mopping the floor. She saw the eternal value in each person, and she encouraged us to do the same.

Not only did Karla see people, she listened to them with her head and her heart. Pam said, "I hold a lot in. Karla always took the time to draw out the pain in my heart. I felt like I could tell her anything and she would always love me, just the way I am."

And then came Karla's words. Her words—both her spoken ones and written ones—packed a wallop and were always encouraging. During those final weeks, Karla's primary means of communication with those she had lived with was through letters. In response to Pam's concern about the media's comments questioning her sincerity, Karla wrote:

> Pamie, bad press does not scare or offend me. God was, is, and always will be in control. It's all about glorifying Him and doing what He tells us to do—with a pure heart. We can only do our part. While we are apart, His grace would be sufficient for you if you'll surrender your will. What is His will, you ask? Good question. But I do have an answer. His will is to trust Him and His decisions with a peace in our innermost being.

At the end of our time together on Death Row, I knelt down and asked the women to pray for me. Just before we got ready to leave, Mary taped the puzzle pieces together and placed Karla's picture on the wall. I said to the women, "We're proud of you and the way you're standing in the midst of this battle. We'll carry you in our hearts. I'll be back in April."

❖ ❖ ❖

In her final video, Karla had spoken words that felt like a

commission: "Linda, even in this pain, if God calls me home, I know that you are going to carry this joy out to the world. We know that the world is watching us, and the world needs to see that there is joy in this as well as pain. There is a pain from loss, a selfish kind of pain, and then it is a wonderful gain, too. You know that I'm going home to be with the Lord, so I'm trusting in your hands to carry that message of joy to the world for me."

My first interview was scheduled the day after I returned to Wisconsin. One of the local television reporters came to my home. We were sitting next to each other on my couch, with the cameraman videotaping from across the room. The reporter was sensitive to my obvious grief, and asked me, "What was the hardest thing for you about the execution?"

Forgetting about Karla's mandate, I began telling her what it was like to have someone so young, full of life and energy, die—what it felt like knowing she was going to be executed and I couldn't do anything to stop it. At that point I started to cry. Then I talked about the tremendous grief that her cellmates and others in the institution experienced.

Shortly after that interview, Karla's words—her message of joy—hit me like a ton of bricks. I knew I had wanted to communicate the message of joy during that interview, but I had gotten stuck in the grief. That night, as I turned on the news, I was relieved when technical problems eliminated the sound of my voice. You could see me talking, but there was no sound. Dallas and I broke into laughter. But that interview was a signal. From then on, I stayed on target.

✦ ✦ ✦

While I was with the women on Death Row, a funeral service was held for Karla in Houston. The *Houston Chronicle* covered the ceremony:

> About 40 people attended her private service at a chapel in Forest Park Lawndale Cemetery in southeast Houston.
>
> The quiet open-casket service on a raw and wet afternoon stood in stark contrast to her Tuesday execution, which drew hundreds of people and more than 200 reporters from around the world to the prison in Huntsville. The service lasted nearly two hours as each mourner took a moment to talk about Tucker and her life.
>
> They included Tucker's husband, Dana Brown; Ronald Carlson, brother of one of her two murder victims, Deborah Ruth Thornton; and J. C. Mosier, the former Houston police detective who helped crack the case 15 years ago.
>
> Mosier said the Rev. Lloyd Maddoux of First Assembly of God in Conroe and prison chaplain Jim Brazzil gave eulogies.
>
> One of Tucker's attorneys, George "Mac" Secrest, then said a few words about the woman who became the focal point for a renewed debate on capital punishment.
>
> "I thought he spoke beautifully about their relationship and how much she meant to him," Mosier said.

He said each member of the audience was then asked to deliver a few words about Tucker.

"The people that knew her got up and talked for a few minutes, mostly to say what a big impact she had had on their life," Mosier said. "There were really some quite eloquent things said by people and it was very interesting to hear."

After the service, about 20 mourners gathered in the cold and rain at the gravesite not far from the chapel. Before the gravesite service ended, Tucker family members asked that police order reporters positioned several yards from the grave to leave the cemetery.

A Houston police officer then told photographers and reporters to leave or face arrest for trespassing.

They left.

Moments later, Tucker's silver casket was lowered into the ground and covered with earth.

The burial plot was left unmarked.

Although I was unable to attend the ceremony, I wanted to visit the cemetery, as well as the nearby Harris County Jail where Karla had given her life to Jesus Christ. I could take Karla's message of joy to her sisters behind the walls there. The setting was familiar as my friend Donna and I walked into the jail. Doors clicked shut with a loud, distinctive thud. Guards sat behind bulletproof windows, with only a small, screened, eye-level opening into which I could speak.

I approached the Master Control window. "We're here to see Cheryl Archer."

After relinquishing our drivers' licenses to the guards, we sat down and waited. Within a few moments a door opened and a beautiful woman, with big blue eyes and blonde hair held back in a barrette, approached us.

"Hi, I'm Cheryl. You must be Linda."

Cheryl exuded peace, a rare commodity in a jail. We hugged each other and began walking toward the elevator. We got off on the third floor, heading toward her office. The inmates sweeping the floor, carrying trays, or being escorted to another floor, were dressed in orange pants and v-necked shirts.

We made a brief stop in her office, where she showed us a poster Karla had mailed her. Sparrows formed the face of Christ. Written underneath were the words, "Not one sparrow falls to the ground without the Father knowing."

Cheryl told us, "I had just arrived home from the funeral emotionally drained. Inside my door was a long tube, addressed to me. I recognized the handwriting—it was from Karla. I sat down and opened it, unrolling the poster. It was so like Karla, reminding me of God's plan."

After looking at other pictures, we went back to the elevator, exiting at the eleventh floor. "I'm playing the video of Karla you mailed me for the women," Cheryl said as we entered the room.

About thirty inmates were sitting on picnic-type tables facing the television. They glanced up as we walked in, but quickly went back to watching the video. When it ended, Cheryl walked over and turned the TV off and introduced me. I greeted them and told them briefly about my relationship with Karla. "Harris County Jail is where Karla was incarcerated after her arrest," I began. "This is also the place where her life was radically transformed. Isaiah 45:3 says, 'I will give you the treasures of darkness.' Karla was a treasure, in the darkest place at the right time. God's light shone through her. But you are a treasure too."

I knew that God had used the video to open their hearts. Once again the Holy Spirit filled the room and they began weeping as I told them that they, too, could experience the same joy Karla had talked about.

❖ ❖ ❖

The next morning Donna, Cheryl, and I purchased five beautiful, long-stemmed roses to place on Karla's grave. Because we knew how much Pam and Frances wanted to be with us, we purchased two roses on their behalf. Not only did we want to place the flowers on the grave for them, we also wanted to assure them that they would not be forgotten in the event of their execution.

Cheryl drove to the enormous cemetery through intermittent showers. I got out of the car and began walking past hundreds of gravestones. As I walked, I thought about the last time I saw Karla. She was radiant, alive. When I had placed my cheek against hers, knowing she was going to die in just a few days, I had felt tremendous sorrow. But then, through this past year, I also saw God's sovereignty as I worked through the grieving process.

Now, though, as I walked I wondered what my reaction would be when again I faced the stark reminder of her death.

After battling the heat and mosquitoes for about two hours, I saw a stone marker: Carolyn Moore Tucker. It was Karla's mother's grave. Overwhelmed, I knelt down and put my hands on the marker. I was close to the end of my search. I knew that Karla's grave was nearby.

Stunned, I knelt there for a few more minutes. Then I began crawling, looking carefully at every nearby stone. My fingers outstretched, I moved slowly across the damp grass, unconcerned if my white pants were being stained by the wet ground. "Unless a kernel of wheat falls into the ground and dies, it remains only a single seed (John 12:24)." Karla and I had talked about that Scripture many times. Now I was actually touching the ground where Karla's body, so like a precious grain of wheat, was placed.

Moving forward, I saw the plaque: "Karla Faye Tucker, November 18, 1959—February 3, 1998." I called out to Cheryl and Donna, "I found it! I found it!" They brought the flowers over. As I slowly placed them on her marker, familiar words rang in my heart: "He is not here—He has risen!" Christ's resurrection made Karla's eternal life with Him possible. I had known and believed she was with the Lord, yet suddenly the joy of that reality flooded me. The gravesite that I thought to be a symbol of Karla's death became instead a recognition of Christ's Life.

Kneeling, I praised God for redeeming Karla, redeeming me, redeeming the women on Death Row and all who call on Him. I praised Him because in the middle of our sin and grief we can hold to His promise: "You have made known to me the path of life; You will fill me with joy in your presence, with eternal pleasures at your right hand" (Psalm 16:11).

Epilogue

It has been over eight years since Karla entrusted this message of joy into my hands. It seemed to me an impossible task to take her message to the nations. But God has a detailed plan that is still in the process of unfolding. My role is simply to listen and to follow His lead. Here's how the Lord's work has continued since this book was first published.

In early 2003, God started tugging at my husband, Dallas, and me to move to Texas. The prison ministry there was expanding, and I was already teaching a study in San Antonio. We were developing deep relationships in Texas, and we felt a spurt of joy and expectancy about the move. However, we were leaving behind thirty years of relationships with family and friends in the Midwest.

One morning, during my time with Jesus, a verse leaped off the page: "Blessed are those who trust in the LORD and have made the LORD their hope and confidence. They are like trees planted along a riverbank, with roots that reach deep into the water. Such trees are not bothered by the heat or worried by long months of drought. Their leaves stay green, and they go right on producing delicious fruit" (Jeremiah 17:7–8, NLT). I smiled as I wrote "Texas" in my Bible next to that passage, thinking about the long, hot summers ahead and the difficult adjustments we were about to make.

Our marriage has been a forty-three year work in progress. We are friends, lovers, and co-laborers for Christ.

That August, a week before we were to move, Dallas was diagnosed with aggressive cancer on the floor of his mouth. Our house in Wisconsin was already sold and we had purchased a house in Gatesville. We had boxes ready to go, with U-Hauls and drivers in place. So with the help of wonderful friends, our earthly possessions were moved and unpacked in Texas. Just after the move, I joined Dallas in Houston, where he was undergoing tests at the University of Texas M. D. Anderson Cancer Center.

As Dallas and I walked this new journey, we knew love like we'd never experienced before. One beautiful afternoon, between tests and appointments, we went to the ocean and danced in the sand.

Then in October my life partner underwent a twelve-hour surgery during which the doctors removed the floor of his mouth and a portion of his tongue. This certainly was not the call we had envisioned. So *this* was the heat and the long months of drought. We felt like we were on a stretcher and needed stretcher bearers. Some of the precious friends involved in Karla's journey carried us. In particular, Art and Aileen Jones welcomed me into their home in Houston and drove me to and from the hospital.

When Big D was released from the hospital, the Joneses took us to their farm, where Aileen gave me a quick course on wound care. When Dallas was ready, Mary Alice and Charlie Wise drove us to Gatesville. They brought us strength, comfort, and practical help as we settled into our home in late October. Meanwhile, the inmates at Mountain View Unit in Gatesville prayed daily for a miracle in Dallas's life.

On our first Christmas Eve in Texas, Dallas spoke at the Woodman State Jail in Gatesville to those who had carried him on the stretcher of prayer. The place was packed with women. We gave out *Karla Faye Tucker Set Free*, and many came

The women at Woodman State Jail praying for Big D.

227

to Christ. We saw again that much suffering produces a great harvest.

We didn't know then what a long road lay ahead of us as we continued to battle Dallas's cancer. Chuck Colson writes in his book *The Good Life*, "Out of suffering and defeat often comes victory." Two months ago, we were told that Dallas has tumors on both lungs and there is no treatment.

The week after this most recent diagnosis, we stood together at Mountain View, in God's House of Freedom, where we have ministered for nearly twenty years. We had a family meeting with the inmates there. Dallas talked about the answers to prayer we have experienced as a result of this struggle.

"We have learned so much about love and sacrifice. I never knew my wife loved me like she does. We would not have chosen this walk, but we have grown through it. Now I have a prayer request. I'd like us to pray that God heals me. This is my request; it is not a demand. Over the years we have learned that God is God and we're not. My life is in His hands."

As the evening progressed, we found ourselves kneeling at the same altar where the women in white had knelt on so many other nights. Every woman was out of her seat with hands extended toward Dallas. Tears streamed down their faces as they passionately cried out to God for their friend. Never have I felt greater love than through this suffering. Jeremiah was exactly right. In the heat and drought our leaves are green and there is delicious fruit.

✦ ✦ ✦

We have seen this truth in the lives of others as well. Again and again we hear how Karla's life story has brought others joy and freedom. This month we received a letter from a psychologist in Ohio. He wrote:

> I am overwhelmed with what God is doing through your book and Karla's life and death. My tradition has not been to shout praises, but I can truly sing in the quiet of my heart, "Praise the Lord for His unfathomable love, mercy, and forgiveness!" God is using Karla to reach so many people—even me. I hope to meet her at the gate someday.

An inmate from a state prison in California sent us this letter:

> I picked up *Karla Faye Tucker Set Free* in the chapel library. Karla's message that life is not about us has gotten through to me. For the first time I know what it means to be redeemed. Every time I break a bondage, every time I get through a hardship, I am redeemed. And I am learning what it means when Jesus says He loves me. Karla's story has made this possible.
>
> I've been incarcerated since 1980. I was sixteen years old when I committed my crime. I'm now forty-two years old. I've never been as brave as

Karla. She did her time with love, dignity, and humility. But with God's love and Karla's model I can live a different life. Karla has taught me to be concerned about my victim's family and not myself.

Over and over we hear and see the results of a life sold out for Jesus. Even though Karla was executed, her story continues to change lives.

Karla's story also continues to have a tremendous impact on those of us who knew her personally. Frances and Pam traveled difficult roads after Karla's death. Even so, their own stories reflect the presence of God—and the good He brings in the midst of pain.

Karla, Pam, and Frances learned the meaning of true friendship in the years they spent together on the old Life Row.

Frances Elaine Newton

Frances missed her prayer walks with Karla. She also missed the old Life Row. Shortly after Karla's execution, the women were transferred to the multipurpose building where Karla was housed prior to her execution. Security was extremely high after seven men escaped from a maximum security unit in Huntsville. Frances remained steady even though she spent most of her time in her cell. Seldom, if ever, did I hear her complain during our visits.

"God always has and always will have a remnant," she said. "He is able to see me through this."

On Thursday, July 1, 2004, Frances was taken to the Harris County Jail in Houston, Texas. She was placed in a holding tank. The officers handed her a purple wristband, indicating that she would be placed in isolation.

In a letter to me she wrote:

> I ended up in an area with about twenty women. We'd left Gatesville in the middle of the night, and I had not eaten in about ten hours. Charlene, a young inmate who was expecting a baby, gave me some of her food. We spent about eight hours together. During those hours, questions came up about the sixteen years I'd spent in TDC [Texas Department of Corrections] and how much time I would actually do. I tried to evade their questions, but as they got more specific I told them that I was on Death Row.

This opened the door. Charlene had read
Karla Faye Tucker Set Free. The next four hours
were spent with questions, reflections, and crying.
I think several inmates will receive Jesus as Lord.
As we were being called out by tank assignments,
we all thanked each other and hugged one another.
Charlene and I were the last two out. I came to
my tank first and she was about to walk off alongside the deputy. But she turned back and gave me
a fierce hug. "I read Karla's story twice and I know
God was with her," she said. "God will be with you
also, Frances."

The next day, Frances received her first execution
date—December 1, 2004. We had great hope it would
not take place. There were many unanswered questions
about her case, and Frances had always maintained her
innocence. Her first state-appointed attorney has been
the subject of many debates, as sixteen of his clients
received the death penalty, and he has been disciplined
five times by the state bar of Texas. Her second attorney
died while working on her appeal, and she was not notified.
When the appeal was not filed in 2001, a judicial watch
group noticed the error and contacted her. As more was
revealed about the shoddy way her case was handled, it
came to the attention of the Texas Innocence Project.
After reviewing some of the questions about the crime,
new attorneys on the case began working long hours, trying
desperately to get a retrial. These attorneys worked pro

bono, with a deep passion for truth. However, a delay was all it bought us.

On November 30, 2004, we arrived at the Comfort Inn in Huntsville, Texas. We had come a day before the execution with Mary Alice and Charlie to pray and to have one more visit with Frances. At noon the next day, we walked into the Hospitality House, located several long blocks from the prison, to wait with her family. They had just returned from their visit with Frances at the Walls Unit, where Death Row inmates are housed the day of the execution. I spoke with Frances's mother, Jewel Nelms, a soft-spoken woman full of faith and conviction. Frances had so many of her mother's good qualities. Jewel seemed unmoved. At one point she said, "I'm just sitting here waiting for God to give me my miracle."

Frances had told me about her sister, Pam, who is a nurse at M. D. Anderson Cancer Center, the place of Dallas's treatment. That afternoon I spent the most time with Pam. After the chaplain prepared the family for viewing the execution, Pam told me, "I've seen the same look on the faces of family members of cancer patients as I see on my family this afternoon." I'd spent long hours in the intensive care unit and I'd witnessed that look as well. Pam and I became intimate allies, both wanting desperately for our family members to survive.

It was nearly 4:00 p.m. and the execution was scheduled for 6:00 p.m. Aileen Jones was with Frances at the Walls Unit. She was her spiritual adviser and could stay until two hours before Frances's death. Suddenly the door opened and Aileen burst in, shouting, "The governor has granted us a 120-day reprieve!" Joy erupted, and we cried and hugged each other. Frances was immediately taken back to Mountain View.

Frances lived her days on the row as a quiet, faith-filled believer. How we miss her sweet smile.

Three days before Christmas, Dallas and I were back at the cancer center. Pam had been tracking our schedule on her computer and surprised us at the head-and-neck clinic. She already knew we were battling a recurrence. After hugging us, she told us her plans to visit Frances the next day. "Frances and I will pray for you. After our visit I'm going to Mary Alice and Charlie's for a prayer meeting for both you and Frances."

In February 2005, we went to visit Frances before

leaving for Seattle, where Dallas would undergo a month of neutron therapy at University of Washington Medical Center. (Neutron is much more powerful than other forms of radiation.) Frances and Dallas talked freely about death and heaven.

"I want to live," Big D said. "I want to see my grandchildren grow up. I want to be with my wife and my family. But I am also ready to die. Death is like walking through a door and taking a step across into another room. We say good-bye to our family and friends here and hello to those who are already in heaven." I felt a deep sadness that night. I didn't want to let either Dallas or Frances go.

The following day, Frances sent us a card that read, "'Now unto him that is able to do exceeding abundantly above all that we ask...' When you can't, He can. I praise God for your healing, Big D, and I love you and Linda very much."

By God's grace, rather than 120 days, we had nine more months to be with our precious Frances. Our son, Terry, and his wife, Jean, left their jobs in August 2005 to join us in the ministry. They encouraged Frances, reminding her that their lives were different because of her. They reminisced about the many miracles they had experienced on the Row. One afternoon they sang, "I Can Only Imagine," a wonderful song about heaven. Then they made up their own words. Frances laughed as Terry sang about her dancing for Jesus. Then Jean reminded her that Karla would be waiting by the gate.

On September 14, 2005, Frances Elaine Newton joined Karla in that great crowd of witnesses. Her family, along with Aileen Jones, viewed the execution. Charlie and Mary Alice, who were her spiritual parents, mingled with those outside the Walls Unit.

I had driven Frances's parents to the walkway to enter the prison. Then I walked among the crowd. A large clock reminded us that the hour was fast approaching. I felt numb and nauseated. There were prayer warriors and reporters milling about. Protesters shouted, "Free Frances!" Guards stood at attention to keep the crowd in control.

One young protester walked over and asked me how I knew Frances. He thanked me for being there and wanted to hear about her final hours. I told him of our phone call a short while before. Frances knew that Jesus was with her, and that was enough. Before saying good-bye, she quietly challenged me to keep running the race and telling the Life Row story.

I cried so many tears that night as I marked off another mile on my long journey home.

Pam Perillo

Pam Perillo is serving a life sentence at Mountain View Unit in Gatesville. We see each other every Wednesday evening in the chapel during Celebrate Recovery, a Christian-based twelve-step program dealing with hurts, habits, and hang-ups. Terry is the worship leader, and Dallas leads Pam's small group. We have over twenty years of history with Pam and have experienced many challenges together. Now she is praying for Dallas as he fights his cancer battle.

Pam has a profound influence on the younger inmates. She encourages them to participate in programs and is serious about her job as a peer counselor. In that role she addresses issues, such as AIDS awareness, Hepatitis C prevention, job training, and the Safe Prison Program.

Her son, Joseph, has graduated from Texas A&M and is now married to his college sweetheart. They write and visit as often as possible. In fact, Joseph has visited monthly since he was six years old; he is Pam's best friend.

Pam was disappointed with God after Karla's death. It took several years for her to work through some hard issues. She had to decide whether to surrender to a God who didn't answer her prayers as she'd like and One whose ways are not always understood. Over the years, she slowly opened her heart again. Then she faced a new crisis of belief. Pam was in our Bible study shortly after Frances received her first execution date. Frances was going through the same material on believing God in her own study with Mary Alice and Charlie on Death Row.

Pam fasted and prayed. But again the execution took place and again it broke our hearts. I spoke at the Mountain View Chapel the Sunday following the execution. It was our memorial service for Frances. Seeing Pam at that service was heart-wrenching. Yet her years of incarceration and her new strength in the Lord Jesus enabled her to endure the pain. She had many of the same questions, but the answers didn't matter anymore. We talked about the fact that God is good—even when things don't go as we want them to.

Every now and then Pam and I have a private moment. Once we talked about her feelings about still being alive after Karla and Frances were executed. We talked about the whys of life and the fact that there are questions that we have no answers for. She wanted to know that I am glad she is alive. I assured her that I am very grateful for her and can see God working His purposes through her life.

Then there are the other times we talk about those wonderful days at the old Life Row. I tell her of the world-

This is the sitting room where Pam spent many hours with her son, Joseph.

wide impact the women on that Row have had; she tells of an inmate whose life was recently changed by this book. And then we look forward. Pam's goal is to be productive and fulfill her purpose. Her dream is to be paroled one day soon. In the meantime she is given *life*... and she is using that life to serve Him.

✦ ✦ ✦

I receive letters almost daily from people who have read Karla's story and understand the good news in a way that releases them to face the challenges of life. Since writing this book, I've had opportunities to go to South Africa and tell of the Lord—our Joy Bringer. I've been in prisons and squatter camps and made wonderful new friends.

I met a photographer from the *Milwaukee Journal-Sentinel* who read *Karla Faye Tucker Set Free*. As a result, Liz wanted to come to the prison and do a story. She especially wanted to talk with Frances, who likely would be the next woman executed. Frances was eager to talk about her deep friendship with Karla and how their friendship led to her intimacy with God. Then an amazing thing happened. This gifted professional photographer surrendered her agenda and began sharing her past with Frances. Frances listened to her with a deep peace and hope that intrigued Liz.

And so in the middle of Liz's project, she was ambushed by Jesus. She even traveled with me on one of my trips to South Africa where I spoke at a women's conference.

At the close of that particular conference I ended with a DVD of Karla signing the song by Ray Boltz, "Thank You." You could see radiant joy in Karla's face as in her mind's eye she pictured people coming one by one into the kingdom. In my heart I thought, *Karla, that's you! Liz is here because of your story. People are entering heaven because you believed God. Your prayer is answered: He is receiving glory.*

As you and I continue to face the unknowns of life, God offers us hope. Jesus is our bridegroom and in His presence is fullness of joy. Together, let's wait with anticipation for the day when we will meet Him at the gate.

My lover said to me, "Rise up, my beloved, my fair one, and come away. For the winter is past, and the rain is over and gone. The flowers are springing up, and the time of singing birds has come, even the cooing of turtledoves. The fig trees are budding, and the grapevines are in blossom. How delicious they smell! Yes, spring is here! Arise, my beloved, my fair one, and come away." (Song of Songs 2:10–13, NLT)

LINDA STROM
Gatesville, Texas
July 2006

Psalm 91: God's Umbrella of Protection Do the latest statistics on cancer, heart disease, and other medical conditions send a chill down your spine? Do thoughts of terrorist attacks and chemical warfare cause your heart to skip a beat? What about all the natural disasters that strike in unexpected places? Indeed — do you sometimes wonder if there is any safe haven anywhere in the world in which you might someday want to hide? If any of these things have ever troubled you, this can be one of the most important books you will ever read! In Psalm 91, the author's highly revealing, biblically based examination of the blessings God promises will open your heart, strengthen your spirit, and revitalize every aspect of your life!

Psalm 91: God's Shield of Protection—Military Version

My Own Psalm 91
—Children's version, *Also available in Spanish*

The Cross Pin
(shown mounted on card)

To request books or cross pins, or for more
information, please contact:
The 1687 Foundation
P.O. Box 1961, Sisters, OR 97759
info@1687foundation.com
541.549.7600 tel•541.549.7603 fax